250-45

**Organizing an Urban
School System for
Diversity**

Organizing an Urban School System for Diversity

144288

A Study of the Boston School Department

Joseph M. Cronin
and
Richard M. Hailer

Lexington Books
D.C. Heath and Company
Lexington, Massachusetts
Toronto   London

In Appreciation

John Kerrigan, the School Committee
Chairman who proposed the study

Dr. William Ohrenberger and
Dr. William Leary, superintendents
who acted on the recommendations

The Advisory Council on Education
and the
Danforth Foundation who supported
the study along with the **City of Boston**

Contents

List of Figures

List of Tables

Foreword

Until the late 1920s the best school systems in the country were found in our great cities, and among these Boston was tops. Growth and shifts in population, technological developments, and political and social change have placed so much stress upon Boston's schools as to require the major concern of citizens everywhere. It is not that quality of the organization and staff of the Boston school system has deteriorated; it is the conditions in which they operate that have so rapidly changed and in some cases deteriorated; it is the complexity and magnitude of the problems which the Boston schools face that demand greater resources and new organization and approaches.

From its inception the Advisory Council on Education has been concerned with the problems of urban education. Not since 1944 were the structure and problems of the whole Boston school system studied. Thus the council in 1969 readily agreed to fund to the extent of $47,000 the request of the Boston School Committee for a study of its school system in accordance with a proposal from Dr. Joseph M. Cronin of Harvard University. The council is gratified that the effort is a collaborative one with the Boston School Committee which contributed $12,000. A portion of a Danforth Foundation grant to Dr. Cronin for study of urban school decision-making was also made available for this study. The council is grateful to McBer and Company (formerly the Behavioral Science Center) for housing, accounting for, and making available its considerable research resources.

The study is broad and deep. Dr. Cronin and his associates spent little time placing blame, and they praised only a few of the admirable developments. They have found that the schools are not sufficiently responsive to the variety of people in the varied neighborhoods. They have found that the policy-making practices of the school committee and the governing procedures of the administration are not sufficiently productive in engendering change and assuring the full range of educational programs required for Boston's children and youth.

In analyzing the problems and in defining new policies, structures, and practices, Dr. Cronin and his staff early and constantly involved Boston's administrators and teachers in the search. This involvement revealed that they generally desired change and improvement.

Perhaps the most controversial recommendation is to enlarge the Boston School Committee and amend the manner to its election. The care with which legislators and Boston's leaders and citizens consider and react to this recommendation will be a measure of their concern and wisdom.

While the focus of this study is Boston, the advisory council believes that its recommendations are relevant to many of the cities of the Commonwealth and hopes that each school administration and school committee will examine them carefully.

Thus, with appreciation to the Danforth Foundation, the advisory council transmits this report to its collaborator, the Boston School Committee, to the citizens of Boston and of the Commonwealth, to legislators, and to the State Board of Education. The problems and needs of Boston's children and youth, often disadvantaged, are many. May this study assist citizens and their leaders to see that they are met.

William C. Gaige
Director of Research
MACE

Preface

We hope this report on urban education and especially on the Boston public schools will be used as a yardstick for measuring educational changes in Boston during the 1970s.

Early in 1971 the superintendent and his staff conducted a school department evaluation of progress on implementing the report's recommendations. A team of twenty Harvard faculty members and advanced degree candidates later in 1971 surveyed programs at the one-year mark. Boston and the state had made progress on many fronts:

- Establishing school councils in dozens of Boston schools
- Selecting a student member of the Boston School Committee
- Securing additional federal money for occupational education
- Increasing the number of minority staff members by 75 in one year
- Enactment of a bilingual education act which required an annual census and required the state to pay the extra costs of programs
- Reorganization of the top staff along the lines suggested in this report
- Decentralizing the medical and health services in one of the areas
- Creating a new approach to supervision through staff development

Publication of a separate report by the Task Force on Out-of-School Youth accounted for, or helped generate support for, several of these changes.

Other constructive moves such as the state approval of open campus plans for Boston schools have been credited at least in part to the 1970 report and the section on using the resources of the city, including those of colleges and corporations.

Still other measures—changes in early childhood education, in the election of the school committee and revision of the budget format—generated more attention than action. At the same time, Boston agreed to consider a variety of new approaches. Among those who worked on the 1971 revision was William Leary, who in May of 1972 was selected as the superintendent of schools in Boston.

If the report did result in progress, it was in large part because of strong support from Superintendent William Ohrenberger, Commissioner Neil V. Sullivan, MACE Director William Gaige, Chamber of Commerce Director James Kelso, NAACP President Kenneth Guscott, Larry Kotin of the Boston Education Alliance, House Education Chairman Michael Daly, and dozens of citizens, educators, and school officials. School Committee Chairman James Hennigan and City Councillor Gerald O'Leary led a 1971 fight to enlarge the Boston School Committee, and others have pledged to continue the effort. Walter McCann of Harvard helped link the study to the Boston-Harvard program at the

Graduate School of Education, and Peter Horoschak served as project administrator of the one-year progress report. Jessica Pers edited and updated the report, although the original recommendations are left intact even where they have been implemented.

Joseph M. Cronin
Secretary of Educational Affairs

Introduction

Origins and Scope of the Study

In January of 1969 School Committee Chairman John Kerrigan called for a study to explore the possibilities for greater economy and efficiency in Boston's system management.

Members of the school committee for several years emphasized the increase in the complexity of decisions they must make or review. Federal and state programs grew rapidly. Collective bargaining demands detailed information about programs and personnel categories. Communities and student groups have tried to communicate their interests and concerns to top decision-makers. The physical and social renewal of a great American city has created new opportunities for education of children and adults. Contemporary forces have severely strained the capacities of a governing board designed in 1906 for a less complex metropolis.

The Boston School Committee has periodically reviewed the arrangements it uses to educate Boston's children. The most recent survey, by George D. Strayer, was filed more than twenty-five years ago. Since then the school committee and the school department staff have confronted quite different problems. The school committee has demonstrated its commitment to redesign its structure and mode of organization to prepare students for the future.

The school system requires a more rational and systematic approach to budgeting, staffing, communications, school-community relations, program development and evaluation, administrative staffing and retraining, and other areas of educational decision-making. To alleviate the crisis in urban education, the system requires increased collaboration with other city and state agencies and with private resources and organizations. The many recommendations of this report will have impact mainly on Boston, which includes approximately one-tenth of the total public school population in Massachusetts. These recommendations also apply to medium-sized cities in Massachusetts.

In this study, the staff reviewed the following problem areas:

- The flow of reports and information to the committee from outside agencies and staff
- Evaluation of educational programs and personnel using in part the "deans' study" of the promotion system
- Present treatment of community relations and participation, and the staffing for school-community relationships
- The division of labor and internal distribution of responsibilities to determine which departments and functions need strengthening
- In-service training for administrators at the building level and special offices at school department headquarters

- The potential use of modern management techniques to prepare the budget for review by the committee, city council, and mayor
- The use of the resources of the business community and other agencies to bring about economy and greater efficiency in the system
- Greater sharing of resources among the schools, the recreation department, health, medical, and other community service agencies
- The size, staffing, authority, term, and other characteristics of the school committee
- The organizational structure of the school department, its staffing, academic and nonacademic, and possibilities for greater productivity

The Study Staff

Both the director and associate director of the study were born in Boston, attended high school in Boston, and graduated from nearby universities. Both have taught in Massachusetts school systems and administered educational programs; one was a school principal, the other a Peace Corps director. Members of the study staff live in Boston, have taught in Boston schools, serve on the boards of civic groups and the Model Neighborhood Board, and visited dozens of schools in the process of this study. The staff included teachers, professors and administrators, lawyers, sociologists, clergymen, political scientists, and public administration specialists. Staff members drew on their experience in the school systems of Chicago, Detroit, Philadelphia, and San Francisco. Several were consultants to states and to the U.S. Office of Education. The youngest staff member completed a practice teaching assignment in Boston during 1970. The most senior staff consultant, a former undersecretary of Health, Education and Welfare, served as a school superintendent in five school systems, including Kansas City and Chicago. Faculty members from Boston College, Boston University, Harvard University, Jackson College, Tufts, M.I.T., Northeastern, and Wellesley College served as advisors, consultants and staff members.

The Methods Used in the Study

"We know the problems," said one school official. "Give us some answers." The superintendent clarified this challenge by pointing out that "urban school systems usually respond to problems with specific solutions and therefore piecemeal change; a report can help by offering long-range targets and specific steps to reach them."

Research and data-collection techniques varied:

- Interviews with parents, teachers, students, and principals

- Community in-depth opinion surveys in selected sections of the city
- Interviews with past and present school committee members, city administrators, associate and assistant superintendents, and most directors of central departments
- Questionnaire surveys on organizational problems, school-community relations, and coordination of outside resources
- A survey of the willingness of selected businesses to cooperate with Boston schools

The study staff used data assembled by other study groups and agencies on school personnel practices, high school programs, pupil services, maintenance repair contracts, school attendance, and nonacademic staff. The study did not review existing curricula, student achievement, or projected facilities needs but did include analysis of decision-making on these issues.

Many recommendations reflect findings by a research team which observed the Boston School Committee from October 1967 through summer 1969. This research, financed by the Danforth Foundation of St. Louis and conducted simultaneously in five major cities, will be reported subsequently. The Danforth grant included a stipulation that study findings and insights be shared with local school officials, a function this report performs.

Collaboration with Boston school staff was vital to this study. Both the affiliation of the study staff with McBer and Company and the Massachusetts Advisory Council on Education's insistence that the study be concerned with implementation were instrumental in developing a spirit of collaboration. MACE helped organize an expert study committee of citizens, academics, school staff members, the Boston Teachers Union President, a student, and concerned agency heads. The superintendent designated two liaison staff members, and he held six meetings with the study directors to outline problems and discuss alternatives. The staff asked several school officials to review plans for a series of workshops; this team of school officials became a sounding board which the staff used before workshop plans were final.

The workshops involved more than one hundred Boston school staff members from all levels in discussions of:

- School relationships with outside agencies, especially health centers, hospitals, universities, and business firms
- School-community relations, emphasizing policy changes necessary to deal with parent and neighborhood groups
- School personnel policy and procedures, especially those concerning minority group personnel
- Educational budget-making, particularly the use of program budgeting and evaluation techniques
- Organizational development, strategies to help the school department staff

plan more effectively, set new goals, and develop new structures as they are needed

Boston school staff members used these workshops to consider long-range policies, offer suggestions for solving complex problems, and comment on the study team's ideas. These meetings provided an opportunity for candid discussion of obstacles and change. The ideas of many Boston educators are in this report—one by-product of the collaboration.

The workshop on outside resources stimulated several proposals to the state for vocational education funds for health careers and other programs. Deans from Boston College, Boston State, and M.I.T. made more specific proposals after the university personnel session. To develop new ideas, the staff held several follow-up meetings with business leaders. White and black educators found the frank and open discussion of minority staff recruitment to be constructive and practical. The sessions on budgeting led staff members to further participation in other seminars on state and municipal budget-making. Workshops also provided suggestions for improving teacher training, community relations, and system reorganization. Most important, these discussions indicated that many school system members are willing to try a variety of approaches to educational problems.

1

The City and Its Children

Greater Boston is rich, diverse, and cosmopolitan. Its physical appearance and the community life of its neighborhoods are as varied and distinctive as the many nations from which its people—or their ancestors—have come. Boston's economy is complex; employment opportunities vary, but many demand highly-developed mental and physical skills.

In the midst of changing lifestyles and neighborhoods, Bostonians must maintain a sense of identity. The visitor to downtown Boston, marveling at the new buildings, is reminded by Faneuil Hall or the Old State House that this *is* also historic Boston. The child becoming an adult in our city must understand traditions and shared values as he or she learns to adapt to new demands and opportunities.

During this century, the public schools increasingly have been expected to assume responsibility for teaching skills and values; in fact, schools begin educating children at earlier and earlier ages. Parents send their children to school with mingled hopes and fears—hopes that each child will learn the skills and attitudes needed as an adult; fears that he will not learn them and will not succeed. Millions of American children have found the schools a bridge to satisfying adulthood, but other millions have found them impossible hurdles.

The relative proportion of hope and fear seems to vary with the socioeconomic level of parents. This is not surprising, for the schools have tended, for the majority, to confirm social position rather than to be a means to change it. It can also be a form of self-fulfilling prophecy, for we know that very much of a child's school experience is determined by his and his parents' attitudes toward schooling. Most often, low-income parents seem to want at least as much for their children as middle-income parents do, but they hope for less and fear more what may happen in school. Unfortunately, their children tend to reflect these lowered expectations.

Teachers are equally likely to hope for less from children from low-income families. Thus, they can have a measurable negative effect on the motivation and performance of these children.

Urban school systems in the United States are not meeting the needs of children from low-income families—a disproportionate number of whom, in Boston and many other cities, are black or Spanish-speaking. Urban school systems are not equipping their students with the skills they will need later.

The problem will not be solved without changing both parental attitudes and school operations: parents and others who influence students' attitudes will not

1

become enthusiastic supporters of the school system unless they believe that the system provides quality education. But no strictly educational improvements will work unless parents and community leaders accept them and communicate that acceptance to children. "Community relations" is, therefore, not an adjunct of the educational process of schools but a vital part of it.

Parents also fear that their children will learn the values and manners of "school people" and turn away from family and ethnic community. This fear is also realistic, for teachers and administrators have often felt it their responsibility to help—or to force—children to adapt to the American mainstream by rejecting ethnic distinctions.

This policy, now more than a century old, has not only reduced diversity in our society and created great pressures for "Anglo-conformity," but also it has not operated consistently for children from all ethnic backgrounds. Millions of children have been alienated from old values but not accepted into the American mainstream. The consequences of such confusion can too often be crime and mental illness.

Members of today's second generation, who in Boston are largely Black, Puerto Rican, and Chinese, are unwilling to be treated by the schools as earlier groups have been treated. They ask that schools help children mature according to their respective ethnic standards and, simultaneously, equip them with the freedom and strength they will need in contemporary society. Schools should not ignore family and community backgrounds while offering children new possibilities for the future.

Good, sensitive teaching, which respects each child's ethnic and individual characteristics, is obviously needed. Teachers must use their own personalities and abilities to reach children in creative ways. Furthermore, organizational arrangements must be flexible to serve teachers' and counselors' needs, not administrative convenience. Principals must serve as community leaders. Top administrators must see that as new needs emerge, resources are allocated, staffs trained, and programs developed quickly, and that out-moded school department policies are abandoned without delay.

The recommendations in this report seek to develop a school system which provides an excellent education for each child, with full respect for individual and ethnic differences. A child cannot choose whether or not he goes to school; his life often depends on what school comes to mean to him. He is entitled to the best education a school system can provide.

Boston Parents: The Climate of Opinion

The Boston School Department Study helped support a systematic sample survey of 397 Boston Public School parents.[a] These parents were selected from

[a]This study (by Jeffrey A. Raffel of M.I.T. and now of the University of Delaware) was also funded by the Office of Education and the Danforth Foundation through the Joint Center for Urban Studies, Harvard University, and the Massachusetts Institute of Technology.

both working-class and middle-class neighborhoods and from different ethnic and racial areas in the city. The sample represents the city population fairly enough to permit us to draw tentative conclusions about the concerns and opinions of Boston parents.

The parent sample was selected from ten elementary schools representing different ethnic and racial groups in Boston: working-class Italian, working-class black, working-class Irish, middle-class Italian, middle-class black, middle-class Irish, Chinese, and Jewish parents. All but one of the schools represented have a fairly mixed (racially, economically, or ethnically) clientele of parents. A list of parents was selected randomly from each of the ten schools. Interviewers were instructed to interview the children's mothers or female guardians; 93 percent of the respondents were women.[b]

Table 1-1 shows the wide distribution of backgrounds of the parents sampled. Although the median income reported was $8,000-9,999, a quarter of the sample earned under $6,000 in 1969 and about 17 percent earned over $15,000. In one-quarter of the sample, the head of the household held a white-collar position. The median age of those sampled was thirty to forty years; their median education was through high school.

Over half of the respondents were born in the Boston metropolitan area; over half were Catholics. Racial or ethnic background: approximately one-quarter of the sample was Irish, one-quarter black, and the remainder divided about evenly among Chinese, Italians, and those of mixed or other backgrounds.

Thus, except for a deliberate oversampling of Chinese parents, the sample in many ways approaches estimates of the total distribution of Boston parents.

A Parental Report Card on Boston's Schools

Generally, the parents interviewed expressed moderate satisfaction with the Boston Public School System (see Table 1-2). Although few termed the schools "poor" (9.1 percent), one in six called the system "very good" (16.9 percent). About 40 percent of the sample rated the system as a "good" one. The parents of the elementary school children in this sample were much less critical of the school system than were the sample of Boston respondents in the Boston Area Survey (Table 1-3).[c] Respondents who have children attending Boston schools appear to be less critical of the schools than those who do not have children attending the schools. Moreover, although 16.9 percent of the sample rated the school *system* as very good, 32.5 percent rated their child's particular school as very good.

However, parents spontaneously criticized the quality of Boston junior and

---

[b]A professional survey research firm, Trans Century Corporation, Washington, D.C. was responsible for interviewing the parents. Those interviewed were all local inhabitants.
[c]Boston Area Study-MIT-Harvard Joint Center for Urban Studies, an annual survey of Boston and Metropolitan area citizens.

Table 1-1
Backgrounds of the Parents in the Study Sample

Background Characteristics	Percentage of Sample (N = 397)
Income	
Under $2,000	2.0%
$2,000-3,999	11.8
$4,000-5,999	12.6
$6,000-7,999	11.8
$8,000-9,999	15.9
$10,000-14,999	14.2
$15,000-19,999	8.6
$20,000-24,999	3.5
$25,000 or more	5.5
Don't know, refused, not verified	14.1
Occupational Level	
Professional, official, manager, owner of business	20.9
Salesman, technical	4.8
Skilled worker or foreman	10.3
Semiskilled, clerical, service, protective worker	44.6
Workman or laborer	9.3
Don't know, refused, not verified	10.1
Education	
Elementary school only	9.8
Some high school	26.2
High shool graduation	41.6
Vocational or technical training	9.1
Some college	6.8
College graduation	3.8
Professional or higher degree	2.0
Not verified	0.7
Birthplace	
Boston	43.6
Boston metropolitan	9.6
Massachusetts	2.0
Other U.S.	24.4
Outside U.S.	20.2
Not verified	0.2
Racial and Ethnic Background	
Irish	24.2

Table 1-1 (cont.)

Background Characteristics	Percentage of Sample (N = 397)
Italian	15.4
Black	23.6
Chinese	15.1
Mixed or other	20.1
Don't know, refusal, not verified	1.6
Religion	
Protestant	25.2
Catholic	53.4
Jewish	1.3
Other or none	19.4
Not verified	.7

Table 1-2
Parental Rating of Quality of Education in the Boston Public Schools

Rating	Percentage
Very good	16.9
Good	39.8
Fair	27.5
Poor	9.1
Don't know	6.7

Table 1-3
Parental Rating of Quality of Education in Their Child's Elementary School

Rating	Percentage
Very good	32.5
Good	40.1
Fair	17.9
Poor	6.8
Don't know	2.7

senior high schools, even though the survey did not include specific questions about secondary schools. The secondary school program clearly needs a major overhaul.

Parents were asked if circumstances permitted, where would they send their child to school: the current public school, another public school, a private school, or parochial school. Although over half said they would not have their child change schools, over 30 percent said they would select a private or parochial school (Table 1-4). Again, although one cannot conclude their dissatisfaction is overwhelming, many parents prefer alternatives to the current system.

A Desire for Change

Although a majority of Boston public school parents interviewed rated the school system as fair to good, many expressed a desire for some major alterations in the school system. When they were presented with three alternative structurings of the school system—(1) the present district encompassing the city of Boston (clearly labeled as the present system); (2) a metropolitan district encompassing Boston's suburbs; and (3) a restructuring of the system into a number of community districts—a majority of the respondents preferred a restructuring of the present system (Table 1-5).

Like the organization of the district, the Boston School Committee as it is presently organized appears unsatisfactory to a majority of the respondents (Table 1-6). The respondents are almost evenly split into four groups—those in favor of the present elected committee; those favoring an appointed board; those for an enlarged, community-based board; and those unwilling to make a choice.

One should not rely too greatly on the specific percentages supporting any

Table 1-4
Parental Desire to Send Child to Alternative School if Circumstances Permit

Choice of School	Percentage
Current public	52.9
Another public	6.3
Private	19.1
Parochial	12.6
Not verified	9.1

Table 1-5
Parental Preference for Alternative School District Plans

Alternative Districts	Percentage
Present Boston District	30.5
Metropolitan District	32.0
Community District	22.2
Don't know	15.1

Table 1-6
Parental Preferences for Alternative Types of School Committees

Alternative School Committees	Percentage
Present five-man elected committee	23.7
Appointed five-man committee	25.4
Elected enlarged committee with community representatives	26.7
Don't know	24.2

alternative. The support for each alternative may well be substantially affected by any public campaign to alter the current system. Clearly, however, a majority of this sample of Boston parents is open to changing the governing structure of the Boston Public School System.

Bostonians have been credited with a widespread cynicism toward their city government; the school system has not escaped this feeling of cynicism. The respondents were asked to agree or to disagree with four statements; the first two derived from accepted scales of political cynicism, the latter two from scales of political efficacy. As Table 1-7 indicates, from 50 to 60 percent of the respondents are cynical with a low feeling of efficacy or control in relation to the Boston schools. For example, over 50 percent of those sampled felt that they could not usually "trust the Boston School Committee to do what is right." Apparently a majority of parents do not feel that the system works directly for them. When they were asked if parents should have greater influence in running the schools, two-thirds said yes and fewer than a quarter said no.

Many respondents wish to alter the system's structure and see a change in personnel patterns. When asked who should be appointed to positions in the system, 41.3 percent of the respondents favored limiting appointments to current Boston administrators. But 43.9 percent favored either appointing newcomers or appointing administrators from inside and outside the system.

Specific Likes and Dislikes

Table 1-9 summarizes the frequency of open-ended mentions of various topics when respondents were asked, "what do you like (and dislike) about the ... school?" Of the 657 positive statements about the schools, approximately one-third referred to teachers. Other items were mentioned much less often. Curriculum, including general assessment of the education children are receiving, and school site location were the most frequently mentioned. Over one-quarter (27 percent) of the complaints centered about school facilities and school plant.

Parent complaints reflect the point made earlier: school system policy rather than the school is often a focus of complaints. This area is mentioned most

Table 1-7
The Cynicism and Efficacy of Boston School Parents

Efficacy Statements	Agree	Percentage Disagree	Don't Know
Sometimes the Boston public schools seem so complicated that a person like me can't understand what is going on.	56.7	36.2	7.1
Voting in the school committee election is the only way that people like me can have any say about how the public schools are run.	53.4	37.5	9.1
Cynicism Statements			
Over the years the Boston public school system has paid little attention to what people think when it decides what to do.	57.2	25.2	17.6
You can usually trust the Boston school system to do what is right.	37.3	50.9	11.8

Table 1-8
Parental Preferences for Who Receives Administrative Appointments

Promotion Alternatives	Percentage
Promote only those within the system	41.3
Appoint new people	20.7
Both	23.2
Don't know	14.8

often. Parents view positively those closest to them—primarily teachers—but they view the total system negatively. Only 9 percent of the negative remarks were about teachers. Two of the three negative items—school facilities and school and system policy—are beyond the control of local schools.

We must emphasize the two other points. First, few people complained (3 respondents) about or praised (15 respondents) their school principals. Principals appeared as relatively neutral characters in the school system. Second, fewer than half the people (46.7 percent) reported a specific complaint.

Table 1-9
Specific Parental Likes and Dislikes about the Elementary School

	Percentage of Likes	Percentage of Dislikes
Teachers	33[a]	9[b]
Curriculum	11	8
Location of school	10	0
Facilities and plant	8	27
Parent relations	7	5
Teaching methods	5	3
School atmosphere	4	5
Class size	3	5
School discipline	3	10
System or school policy	3	13
Other	10	14
	N = 657	N = 457

[a]Percentage of the 657 specific items liked
[b]Percentage of the 457 specific items disliked

Parental Preferences in Curricula and Methods

Parents responded most easily and with most involvement to one survey question. Interviewers asked parents how much attention should be given to a long list of topics (e.g., good grooming, pollution, drugs, creative writing) in their children's elementary schools (see Table 1-10). Almost three-quarters supported greater emphasis on drug education, even in elementary school. Second, many parents identified a need for school attention to race relations. Third, parents gave sex education low priority as a subject appropriate for elementary school in Boston.

Several subjects seem to be related. Concern about drugs, proper behavior, loyalty, good grooming, preparation for a job, and study of communism are all more traditional concerns in the social control of individuals. At least 25 percent of Boston's parents believe each of these concerns should be given major attention in the public schools.

On the other hand, a cluster of topics which indicates other priorities—race relations, pollution, Negro history, creative writing, and city problems—are also matters of concern, though only race relations is one of the most popular topics.

Concern about children's behavior is a recurring theme among parents sampled. Table 1-11 indicates parents believe (25.1 percent) that motivating children should be the first goal of elementary schools, but a concern for teaching proper social behavior is a close second (17.0 percent). This sample of Boston parents expressed more concern for teaching desired attitudes and

Table 1-10
Parental Preferences for Attention Given to Various Topics

| Subject | Percentage Preferring a "Great Deal" of Attention Given to the | |
	Subject	Rank
Drugs	71.0%	1
Proper behavior	44.1	2
Loyalty to the country	39.0	3
Race relations	33.2	4
Preparation for a job	32.7	5
Good grooming	27.7	6
Pollution	27.5	7
Black history	26.4	8
Creative writing	22.2	9
Communism	19.9	10.5
City problems	19.9	10.5
Vietnam war	18.6	12
Religion	18.4	13
Sex education	14.6	14
Music appreciation	12.8	15
Irish history	6.0	16

behavior (desire for learning, proper behavior, critical thinking, individual understanding) than for skills and knowledge (basics, information, home and employment skills).

Approximately two-thirds of the respondents favor a greater parental voice in the schools. Parents were asked about ten specific parents roles. Some roles—e.g., helping children with homework—have traditionally been considered a parental perrogative. Others—helping decide how the school spends its money—have not.

As Table 1-12 indicates, parents prefer to have more jurisdiction over their schools by working with (and in) them rather than by making decisions about them. Two-thirds of them want a general say in school decisions. Although fewer than half the parents favor involvement in decisions concerning budget, curriculum, teaching methods, principal hiring, over half favor parental involvement with their children's homework and as aides in their children's schools. Only on disciplinary methods did a majority of parents support a parental decision role.

But the size of even the least popular decision alternative is fairly high; a minimum of approximately one-quarter of the respondents favor a parental role in hiring school personnel. And these percentages may be underestimates,

Table 1-11

Parental Choice of Preferred Primary Goal of Their Children's Elementary School

Teaching Goal	Percentage Selecting Goal as Most Important
Desire for learning	25.1
Proper behavior	17.0
Critical thinking	14.5
Individual understanding	14.2
Basic tools (3 Rs)	12.3
Information	6.7
Home and employment skills	3.4
Don't know	6.8

Table 1-12

Parental Opinions Concerning Role of Parents in Schools and School Decisions

Area of Parent Role	Percentage Favorable
Child's homework	83.9
Volunteer aides (nonpaid)	78.2
Discipline methods	67.0
General say	66.2
Teacher aides (paid)	63.2
Budget	41.1
Curriculum	40.3
Teaching methods	33.2
Principal hiring	25.4
Teacher hiring	23.7

for many parents who did not want a regular role in hiring decisions did want a veto over teachers or principals who did not meet their minimum standards. Many did not favor a permanent parent role but supported a veto role.

2 A School System and Its Programs

The study team found many excellent teachers, several successful parent-school programs, some inspired, forward-looking administrators, and many laudable programs in the Boston schools. The work-study program, the Trotter School and the Educational Planning Center, new art and music programs are among these.

This chapter concentrates primarily on problems in the Boston School Department, especially those problems which hinder the school department's functioning effectively in the situations discussed in Chapter 1. Following general comments, it will describe in detail the changes in roles and organizational structure necessary to make the Boston School Department a wholly effective organization responding to the city's diversity.

Goal Setting. Goal setting receives little attention in the Boston Public Schools now. At least two dozen departments are involved in developing programs, but educational goals appear only in some curricula guides. The amount of time the school committee devotes to matters of educational policy seems to be limited; this demonstrates a lack of long-range educational planning. Commitments like those stated in the superintendent's 1968-69 annual report, e.g., "to serve to the fullest all the children, youth, and adults of the city" and "to educate every child to the maximum of his potential," are laudable but ambiguous, and therefore cannot be evaluated meaningfully. When educational goals are stated, e.g., in the Individual Progress Program and the Elementary Enrichment Program, they are not specific enough to be measured. (Chapter 11 contains a detailed report on planning and evaluation in these Title I programs.)

The formulation of educational goals must take place at three levels—the system, the area, and the school or neighborhood levels. Goals must be conceived explicitly and articulated clearly, e.g. to raise reading scores on a particular test by two grades within six months.

Sensing Relevant Information. To set goals for effectiveness, the Boston School Department must be open to its clients and personnel, and to outside demands and environmental changes. The school department presently lacks adequate mechanisms for acquiring much of the information it requires to function effectively. At present, many parents, principals, teachers, and students feel frustrated in their attempts to gain access to school department decision-makers. The at-large election of the school committee practically insures that candidates from minority groups will not be elected, although their children comprise almost 50 percent of the total school population. No regular communications channels exist that assure everyone in the system access to information about resources. Because of the present hierarchical structure, information tends to flow downward from, instead of upward to, central decision-makers.

Opening to Diversity. The Boston School Department must recognize and utilize the diversity of the city. Student, parent, and teacher advisory councils should be established at the local, area, and city levels. Part of the school committee should be elected on an area basis. Better links to resource centers must be created; universities and experts at state and federal levels should be used as valuable resources. Recommendations for implementing improvements in these specific areas are included in Chapter 13.

Program Administration. The Boston School Department's problem in program administration is its inability to evaluate what it is doing and has done, rather than its actual carrying-out of programs. This results from lack of clear-cut responsibility for decisions and the nonexistence of evaluation mechanisms. A model for evaluation is provided in the chapters on budgeting and on Title I programs.

Program Formulation. The Boston School Department has taken steps to establish the Educational Planning Center and Department of Curriculum Development. According to the 1968-69 ANNUAL REPORT OF THE SUPER-INTENDENT, the department has proposed a resources center and the organization of in-service workshops in cooperation with industry and higher education. In the past the Boston School Department has been isolated from new ideas and therefore has not had alternatives from which to make program choices. In addition to the proposed resource center, teachers and principals should visit other school systems to study the operation of innovative programs. Also more people from outside the system should be consulted to help generate new ideas, and teachers and administrative personnel should receive periodic exposure to new thinking in university courses and in-service training.

Local Decision-Making. Many decisions must be made closer to the school level, and responsibility for decisions must be clearly defined to make program implementation more effective. Directives from Beacon Street are often ignored or carried out half-heartedly. For example, if all principals are given a certain program to incorporate into their schools, those who feel it does not apply to their particular situation are likely to ignore it. Responsibility for decisions about program implementation should be shifted to the area superintendent and principal. These people, and the teachers they supervise, are more aware than many central departments of what applies to the children in their areas.

The Need for Evaluation. Evaluation is the decision makers' key tool. The lack of evaluating mechanisms in Boston is the most serious handicap to the system's effectiveness. New skills and capacities must be built into the school system. This will require hiring people with statistical and research skills; designing, with outside help, an evaluation plan; designing and operating a complete information system to supply data to planners and evaluators; implementing research contracts with outside consultants, designed so that the contractor will be guided by the system's real needs; and establishing a system to interpret evaluation results to guide planners in new policies and programs. An entirely new planning-evaluation mechanism must be devised. This will necessitate organizational change, new hiring policies, and considerable money.

Program Change. The Boston School Department has made significant program changes in recent years. The 1968-1969 ANNUAL REPORT OF THE SUPERINTENDENT highlights many recent curricula innovations from the introduction of a high school social studies program on the Far East to harp lessons at an elementary school. But the system must give more attention to program change in response to evaluation and meeting goals. Effective program change requires the adoption of an entire planning-evaluation process.

To become an effective organization prepared to meet the challenges of change and diversity, the Boston School Department must evaluate, plan, and adapt. The system must adapt to changes in clientele, composition of the city, and the needs of individuals and society. It must plan not only new facilities but new ways to work with other education agencies—museums, the media, employers, and universities. It must evaluate federal and state programs, and its own programs and personnel. This is an ambitious mandate, but Boston parents and Massachusetts citizens are insisting on higher productivity and more effective performance from urban school systems.

Curriculum and Program Development

Most curriculum decisions are both centralized and fragmented. In general, programs are prepared by teachers on a city-wide basis. But at least four associate superintendents can veto parts of a kindergarten-through-grade twelve curriculum. Each level—elementary, junior high, and senior high—has its own superintendent. (Until recently almost all superintendents were veteran principals with forty years or more in the system.) Simultaneously, an associate superintendent for curriculum tried to coordinate program revision. But he usually has other chores—legislative liaison or responsibility for planning.

At the same time each of several dozen directors (Boston has approximately thirty-five) can encourage or slow down curriculum change. Many experienced directors received the bulk of their training in the 1920s and have had only minimal in-service training. Some innovative new programs have been launched— in data processing, licensed practical nursing, and other postwar technologies. But the curriculum of the 1920s and 1930s persists in too many specialized programs.

There are exceptions. The Individual Pupil Progress (IPP) elementary program uses unstructured learning environments and a variety of teaching methods. Teachers use the Botel Reading Inventory to diagnose the learning needs of students in the IPP program.

The school system tests students regularly. Regrettably, from 1967 to 1970 six different national standardized tests have been used in Boston. Therefore, parents, state officials, and evaluators cannot make meaningful before-and-after evaluations. Teachers and principals had no say in this change. The system switched from reporting average achievement scores by grades (e.g., grade 5.6 reading achievement) to stanines, a statistical measure which, although appropriate for many uses, makes comparisons difficult.

Another kind of program evaluation is faculty self-evaluation, followed by team visits from the New England Association of Colleges and Secondary Schools. These reports list physical plant problems, and serious curriculum shortcomings. Many of the comments and recommendations are constructive and inexpensive to implement.

Fortunately, many school officials no longer interpret these reports as criticisms of the system, but instead see them as incentives for improvement. Unfortunately many of the reports are kept in headmasters' offices instead of being released for faculty and parent study, discussion, and action.

Guidelines and materials for the evaluation of elementary, junior high, and middle schools are now available from the New England Association of which Boston is a member.

Program evaluation is more than simply testing academic skills. Urban educators recognize the need for greater attention to "affective education," the feelings and values students develop and the ways in which they work through problems of identity, career, and personal choices. Only a few city school systems (Philadelphia is one) have begun to develop parts of an "affective" curriculum for the urban child, although some of the materials in the "Sesame Street" series also stress similar ideas and useful approaches. City schools must also have the staff and facilities to develop physical competence and sufficient stamina to survive in a competitive urban culture.

Each child needs a profile of test scores and constructive comments, which each year can be shared and discussed with parents (and the child as he or she matures). Each school needs a profile of test scores and other information on achievement and needs that can be shared with faculty and parents for discussion of new approaches and program revision. Compiling raw or aggregate data is not enough.

Decisions about new goals and new curriculum can be made on several levels.

Each child is different. Most schools should be different. For example, areas of the city vary in their needs, in the percentage of bilingual children or science-oriented students; schools should reflect this diversity.

Some children need to be set free from the school for a while—for a few days, or a few weeks, or a few years. Boston's work-study program begins to change the pattern of 9 to 3 daily schooling, but a student must be a potential dropout to qualify. The compulsory school attendance law is too strict; school officials and courts can exclude a child for negative conduct but cannot prescribe as an educational course a full month or year on the staff of a department store, an aquarium, a hospital, or an airport and give academic credit for experience. Educators must concentrate on helping each child experience, absorb, and evaluate his or her own world.

This report includes some immediate, specific suggestions for solving parts of the problems outlined. But all educators, in universities, in schools or in other agencies, must help develop new ways to educate the city child for a postindustrial society, a society which stresses service to man more than the traditional production of material goods. The challenge of defining a totally new urban education falls beyond the scope of this report; it requires the collaboration of scores of cities to develop the ideology, program, and the necessary technology. But the way cities wrestle with this issue can be improved substantially.

Curriculum Development and Supervision

Fifty years ago each major city developed curriculum guides for their courses. Smaller cities and towns often bought these for their own uses. Even in the 1960s, the Learning Institute of North Carolina and other agencies adopted some of Boston's reading programs.

But many new courses now cost millions to produce (several of the modern physics programs cost more than $5 million each) and they involve trial runs, summer workshops at colleges, and the production of texts, films, laboratory equipment, educational games, pamphlets, and other materials. Today, no single school system could possibly afford to develop its own curriculum. City systems now join regional laboratories or specialized centers as Boston has done with the Educational Development Center, largely financed with federal funds, and the Lincoln Filene Center at Tufts.

Cities once adopted a single reading program for grades one through eight, a single social studies program, a single science sequence, and so on. But now children's diverse needs and talents require a variety of options and choices. A city needs, for example, at least the four major biology course options developed by national study committees in the 1960s. Different students require varied approaches to reading.

Children enter school with many thousands of hours of television watching (estimates of inner-city children's viewing time run as high as fifty hours per week) and background never expected of them. Yet today's curricula hardly vary from those used for Irish and Italian immigrant children a century ago.

Some have argued that children who will live half their lives in the twenty-first century need a fundamentally different curriculum—one that stresses the peaceable resolution of human conflict, one that enables a person to change habitats frequently and learn new job skills five or more times in a career, and one that develops the emotional stability and aesthetic sensibility needed to survive and enjoy urban living. The classics will continue to have a place in this curriculum, but elementary and intermediate grades may need to provide substantially different offerings, very few of which have been developed.

Boston has begun to make changes in the field of supervision. Until 1969 one set of supervisors observed and evaluated provisional teachers and another set worked in the same building with probationary teachers. One set worked in elementary education and another set for personnel. Neither worked with the new office of curriculum development, a staff which coordinated new programs in social studies.

In 1969, the office of curriculum development developed new curriculum guides which emphasized the contributions and history of blacks and minority groups in America. Black staff members from the Boston School Department and the Lincoln Filene Staff selected materials. Several senior high schools began to use the curriculum immediately, demonstrating the usefulness of collaboration between school staff members and university personnel. However, any written course guide rapidly becomes obsolete. Principals are justifiably critical when outstanding teachers are taken from the classroom to develop new guides. Teachers should develop curricula in the summer and then test and refine them during the school year.

The supervisory staff should not continue as a separate, centralized group. Each area superintendent should coordinate a group of from two to four helping teachers who should work on curricula and assist teachers. The central staff approach can stifle creativity. Specifically, decisions to retain a teacher, to recommend one for tenure, and to recommend another for transfer or reassignment should be made by the principal and assistants of elementary, junior high, and intermediate schools. Headmasters and senior high department heads already enjoy significant authority over these functions. Advice and support as it is required should come from school colleagues and the staff in each area office.

Recommended for Boston

- Curriculum and supervisory staffs should work cooperatively under an associate superintendent for curriculum and instruction and with the associate superintendent for staff and organizational development. The merger of these functions centrally should be considered.

- Principals and headmasters should assume responsibility for teacher evaluation and retention with assistance from resource teachers on the area superintendent's staff.
- Curriculum guides should be replaced by brief outlines of scope and sequence in courses requiring continuity between levels. The major activity of curriculum and supervision staff shall be materials evaluation and assistance to school faculties.
- Schools in each area should be used to refine, test, and adapt alternative programs and teachers should visit these model schools. The idea behind the Boardman-Trotter subsystem is sound—schools should develop different ways to instruct children and then accept the method which is best suited to the school and environment.
- The curriculum and instructional staffs in areas such as fine arts and music (aesthetics) and physical education ought to be gradually expanded because these subjects are vital to the survival of body and spirit in Boston. Special teachers for these subjects, however, should not be assigned centrally. They should be assigned first by area and eventually to each elementary school, one specialist in each field for every 1,000 children.

Audio-Visual and Libraries

Radio and film techniques are used mainly as adjuncts in the education process. Recently, largely because of the National Defense Education Act, the overhead projector and electronic tape have become more widely used in science, math, and foreign language classes.

Until recently, Boston school libraries existed only in senior high schools and half of the junior high schools. Yet, several senior high schools had only limited library facilities. Even the Boston Latin School Library was closed for several months because it lacked an acceptable school librarian. Most elementary schools in Boston, as in other large cities, did not have libraries until the Elementary and Secondary Education Act provided additional funds. More than 100,000 library books have been purchased under Title II of ESEA.

For many years the Boston School Department has maintained an administrative library at school committee headquarters, which contains textbooks, reports, and curriculum guides from other cities. However, many teachers cannot travel to the Beacon Street library to get a book or pamphlet or scan the catalogue.

Ten years from now, television and computers may become more important in the instructional process. Because of "Sesame Street" and the "Electric Company," many people have recognized the impact of television on childhood learning. The widespread availability of computer-assisted instruction, however, seems perhaps a decade away. In coming years, teachers must learn to use new technology and not fear that they will be "replaced" by machines.

Recommendations

- Boston should continue to strengthen its audio-visual services, especially in teacher training and the development of a materials center where tapes, filmstrips, records, and projector material can be gathered.
- Libraries should continue to grow with the help of school volunteers and federal funds. The school committee should make sure library funds from all sources are not cut. The several librarians-in-charge can continue the expansion program, helped by some 450 volunteers and additional paid aides recruited from the neighborhood.
- The central administration library should be designated an educational information center to be computerized and tied closely to curriculum materials evaluation. The model schools in each area should also have new curriculum materials, films, and other multimedia collections, chosen by teacher committees.
- By 1975 the school committee should again review the state of instructional technology and decide whether to combine audio-visual services, libraries and other media into a Department of Instructional Technology. For now, the associate superintendent should retain responsibility for coordination, pilot programs, and frequent evaluation of new developments in this emerging field.

Early Childhood Education

Boston, with St. Louis, pioneered the development of public kindergartens in America during the 1870s. Today, Boston offers two years of kindergarten for 5,509 four-year olds.

In Boston the Headstart Program began under sponsorship of Action for Boston Community Development Program (ABCD), the antipoverty agency. In 1970 the program served almost 1,200 children from low income homes, although fewer than 100 are Spanish-speaking. Day-care centers operate apart from the city's school department. These centers provide rapidly growing educational programs in education.

The Boston Kindergarten Department provides supervision, materials, and curriculum leadership. The staff is separate from elementary supervision, and it assumes no responsibility for day-care centers in the city.

This department should be merged with other elementary programs (supervision or curriculum development) and its jurisdiction redefined as early childhood education with major responsibility for planning educational programs for children three years old or more. The educational component of child-care services is especially important because of welfare reform and the interest of mothers, government agencies, health centers, and firms, in excellent *comprehensive* child programs.

The public schools are geographically and administratively set up to provide day-care services and could be selected as possible sites. Here is one instance in which the neighborhood school can work to enrich the total community.

Placing the day-care center in the school would mean opening the school building to parents. Parental concern for preschoolers should extend to their other children schooled in the same locations. Parental participation is a prerequisite for federal funding of a day-care center; Boston, and most large cities, cannot attempt public early childhood programs without it.

The advantages that federal funding would bring to the city system might offset bureaucratic problems and strains. Pilot programs could include on-the-job teacher training, involving developing a work-study program to train older neighborhood children in child-care techniques.

The school department would need to anticipate and solve many problems before a public school system could assume responsibilities for some day-care programs. The argument against day care—that young children should not be away from their parents, particularly their mothers—is a matter for parents to decide.

Community participation, different from parental involvement, is important. Through the mechanism of the 4C (Community Coordinated Child Care) Committees, agencies and businesses can make contributions of manpower and resources. Massachusetts may designate 4C Committees as the representative group composed of at least one-third parents and one-third public or private agencies of a community. Recognition of these committees would make possible day-care funding from federal, state, and local agencies.

Recommendations

- The Boston Kindergarten Department should transfer its supervisory staff and responsibilities to the area and join the central curriculum department.
- School department jurisdiction over early childhood programs should include educational components of day-care centers, Headstart and follow through programs, and coordination with other agencies. The school department should make special efforts to serve poor families, working mothers, the Spanish-speaking, Chinese, Haitians and other minorities.

Vandalism, Violence, and the Curriculum

During the 1960s Boston schools were vandalized, robbed, and in six instances burned down. The bill for broken windows alone rose from $16,797 in October 1968 to $21,234 in October 1969. Vandalism costs amount to $1.50 per pupil in twelve of the nation's largest school systems.

The Urban Education Task Force appointed in March 1969 by former HEW Secretary Robert Finch discussed the school vandalism problem. They found that school officials and the general public usually respond to vandalism in anger, "not only because of the damage caused and the hostilities expressed but because of the seeming senselessness of the acts." The words "criminal" and "pointless" are often used.

But are the acts totally without meaning? Research in the United States and England revealed that "the highest rates of school vandalism tend to occur in schools with obsolete facilities and equipment, low staff morale and high dissatisfaction and boredom among the pupils."[a] The task force concluded that public anger is justified, but that vandalism is connected to the feelings of frustration and hopelessness in many schools. Recently, vicious attacks on teachers and principals suggests an expansion of this hostility to school.

Some systems have hired armed watchmen, deployed dogs in the school, installed expensive electronic devices, and even used helicopters with searchlights each night. Urban experts warn that such policies will further reduce morale and mutual respect.

As early as 1964 Boston school officials used revised school programs, beginning with Operation Counterpoise, as effective ways to reduce truancy and vandalism. The new program at the Boardman School between 1967 and 1969 transformed student and parent distrust to strong support of the Model Subsystem.

The Boston School Committee in 1968 pledged a "War on Vandals." But most of the vandals are school children; "victory" can be won only by principals and teachers who enjoy the confidence of parents and pupils and who can fight successfully not for rock-proof windows but for interesting instructional materials.

Boston educators have called for modernizing the junior high and senior high curricula, including courses in urban problems, law, the economics of survival, communication, health, technology, and human relations.

Policy, Rules, and Regulations

The latest book of statistics, policies and regulations is dated 1935 and does not even include many important current topics. Two men have tried to codify the

[a](Reprinted in URBAN SCHOOL CRISIS. The Problems and Solutions Proposed by the HEW Urban Education Task Force, Washington, D.C., U.S. Government, January 1970.)

Boston School Committee decisions since 1935 but neither the board of superintendents nor the school committee has considered the work complete enough to publish.

During 1970, a Boston judge expressed amazement that the most recent rule-book was published thirty-five years ago, for lawsuits as well as day-to-day administrative decisions require some kind of policy handbook.

But decisions on "new" issues—corporal punishment, the rights of women teachers, parents and student rights to appeal suspension, and other legal and administrative guidelines—require frequent changing. Perhaps each office needs a loose-leaf policy notebook, with supplementary and substitute pages issued to directors and principals each year as needs arise.

Many of the materials in the 1935 handbook deal with specific sections of the Boston Teacher Exam or establish the elementary school boundary lines which change when a new school is opened. What principals need is an up-to-date listing of the essential policies, statutes, and contracts. Beyond that principals and headmasters need as much flexibility and discretion as possible to meet the diverse needs of their neighborhood and community.

Parents, teachers, and students want to share in making the rules that shape their lives. A mayor's committee in 1968-69 found that several high schools did not have student councils. Some principals call meetings of the Home and School Association at times when one or both working parents cannot attend. Teachers, frustrated by stale faculty meetings, have asked for the right to discuss school policy with principals. A high morale and highly productive urban school system will involve clients and workers in as many decisions as time and the law permit.

3

Roles and Responsibilities

The Area Superintendent

*Original Purpose of the Role of the
Area Superintendent*

In the annual report of the Boston schools for 1966-67, area (or assistant) superintendents were described as "local educational leaders." Since 1966, when the position was established, however, the trouble-shooting aspects of the assignment have so dominated that the area superintendents have had little opportunity to provide leadership for systematic development of educational programs in their areas. Area superintendents need not only authority and responsibility, but also the time and staff assistance to supervise educational planning.

Evolution of the Role

Presently, the area superintendents devote the largest portion of their time to their role as integrator—achieving unity of effort among the major functional specialists in an organization. They facilitate communication between the school system's central offices and building principals. They meet with parents and community organizations, largely to resolve misunderstandings and interpret the school system's program to the public. They attempt to resolve interdepartmental difficulties that affect the schools' operation in their areas. In addition, all of them have been assigned ancillary duties which usually involve supervising some system-wide project, program, or service, such as programs for the Spanish-speaking or mental health agency liaison. Finally, several of the area superintendents spend much of their time trying to locate additional classroom space to accommodate the rapidly growing pupil populations in their areas.

These trouble-shooting and ancillary duties have rapidly overshadowed one of area superintendents' main functions: regular consultation with principals and teaching staffs in each school in their areas.

This change in emphasis resulted primarily from increasing demands which community groups placed upon area superintendents. The area superintendents have effectively performed an essential community relations function. But until the area superintendents can respond to individual concerns of community groups, the school system as a whole will be unable to respond adequately to community pressure.

Parents are concerned that the schools which their children attend are satisfactory. They demand that schools in their areas respond to particular needs of particular groups of children—providing Spanish-speaking teachers, opportunities for independent study, or hot lunch programs. They do not demand that all of the schools in the city adopt the programs which they feel their particular children need. But because of existing centralized policy-making and system-wide program development, area superintendents can rarely deviate from established system-wide curricular programs, personnel staffing policies, or other accepted practices to respond to highly particular needs or requests.

In response to demands that public institutions reflect the diversity of contemporary urban society, many large city school systems have decentralized their decision-making structures. These systems are establishing structures that bring professional responsibility as close as possible to the educational consumer. At the same time they are working out procedures for preserving accountability and coordination to permit systematic educational development. As administrative decentralization increases, planning as a means for preserving accountability becomes essential.

To accomplish this in Boston the assistant superintendents' role should be redefined as an educational leader and planner rather than a system trouble-shooter. By dividing the city into six areas, the school committee intended to bring the management and planning functions closer to the schools. This significant reform must now be carried through to its conclusion.

Obstacles to Achieving Original Purpose

The original purpose of the area superintendent position has not been achieved for a number of reasons. The most obvious is the area superintendents' small staff. Each operates with only one aide, a combination secretary and general assistant. These assistants are unable to provide as much staff support as the area superintendents would need as effective program planners in their areas. Also, assigning system-wide responsibilities to area superintendents has significantly hampered their effectiveness as area leaders. The supervision of system-wide projects or the responsibility for monitoring programs not directly related to the educational program of his area, inevitably takes an area superintendent away from his primary responsibility—leading the principals and teachers in his area.

Other problems develop from the area superintendents' relationships with the central administrative staff and with the principals in their areas. In the formal organizational structure, area superintendents are subordinate to the board of superintendents. They do not have the opportunity to participate in the school system's basic policy formulation. As a result, their needs are inadequately represented when basic policy is being formulated. Also they share with several associate superintendents the authority to supervise principals at each level (elementary, junior high, senior high). Divided authority, even if clearly understood by all parties, denies to both area and associate superintendents the authority each needs to lead school principals and staff. It also confuses, sometimes to the point of inaction, those supervised. Finally, many services the central staff normally provides do not respond to the particular needs of an individual school. If each area superintendent were free to supervise program planning for the particular needs of children in his area (e.g., special education or social studies programs), many of the central service departments would have to develop corresponding flexibility to provide necessary support. That capability is presently not developed in many cases.

Finally, the existing relationship between the area superintendents and principals is not conducive to effective planning. Traditional courtesy maintains that an area superintendent (or anyone else) cannot interfere with a principal's management of his school. Of course, a principal should have the authority to control the educational program in his school. But, more important, a principal must be accountable for his school's program. The area superintendents should raise questions, work with principals as they seek solutions to problems and help them evaluate the effectiveness of school programs.

Relationship of Area Superintendents
to Central Office

Several school systems—in Chicago, Philadelphia, and Dade County, Miami, Florida—have decentralized both operational administration and instructional and supporting services. Each area administrator supervised a relatively large staff of instructional coordinators, pupil personnel administrators, and other educational specialists. The difficulty with this organizational structure is that administrative costs can increase rapidly if each area reproduces the organizational pyramid which formerly existed in one central office.

On the other hand, school systems in New Orleans, Nashville, and Boston have developed decentralized administration of operations but have retained centralized instructional and supporting services. Under this organizational scheme, it is difficult to tailor educational programs to the needs of different areas and individual schools. Service departments tend to develop and implement the same policies throughout the system, giving area administrators and building principals little opportunity to devise different approaches. Ultimately, area administrators tend to become trouble-shooters responding to individual crises, and principals become coordinators of services and programs which are designed in the central office.

Recommendations

The school system must expand its capability for identifying public needs and attitudes and developing responsible educational programs to satisfy them. To do this, area superintendents should participate in the central policy-making, goal-setting process for the entire school system. In addition, each area superintendent must be responsible for developing a detailed educational plan for his area consistent with the system's goals.

Area superintendents should report directly to the deputy superintendent and participate in the system-wide goal-setting process. They should not be encumbered with the system-wide administrative detail that can take up the agenda of school department cabinet meetings. These matters can best be handled by direct contact between the deputy superintendent's assistants and the appropriate associate superintendents. Instead, area superintendents should help define long-range educational plans for the system—work-study programs, more individualized learning, affective learning, or other approaches which the area superintendents, through knowledge of local concerns and needs, feel is necessary.

Area superintendents must participate at the highest administrative level of policy formulation. The present practice of having one area superintendent represent his colleagues at meetings of the Board of Superintendents is too limited, and makes it impossible to hold area superintendents responsible for planning.

Many service departments—curriculum, teacher supervision, and to some extent, the Educational Planning Center and attendance department—would have to provide different services to several areas and schools consistent with the separate plans and goals each had adopted. Recently, the curriculum and teacher supervision departments and EPC have responded to the requests of individual area superintendents and schools to help solve particular educational problems. The demands on these departments for individualized service would undoubtedly increase as the program planning responsibility recommended for area superintendents and principals becomes clearer. In short, areas and individual schools should become consumers of many of the services the central departments provide. As consumers they should have the latitude to select services consistent with their approved program plans. In this way both diversity and accountability will be preserved.

Several areas and schools probably would choose to supplement their programs by using resources outside the school system. Insofar as these choices are consistent with system-wide goals, they should be encouraged. But the development and maintenance of continuing, productive relationships with businesses, museums, universities, and other resources require constant attention. The responsibility for bringing together the needs of the schools and outside agencies should be centralized.

Relationship of Area Superintendents to Principals

Just as periodic goal-setting is necessary for the school system, so should each area establish specific objectives which serve both the system's general goals and the needs of the children and community in the area. This could be accomplished as part of the regular planning process which would involve the area superintendent, his principals, and parent representatives.

Area meetings of principals should do more than communicate decisions down the chain of command. They should be (as they are in some cases) problem-solving workshops and planning meetings. Sometimes only those principals who share a common problem need meet with the area superintendent. Area superintendents must encourage their principals to share problems with each other instead of feeling that to reveal a problem reflects administrative inadequacy.

Each principal should meet with his area superintendent to make certain that the program for his school is consistent with the goals for the area and to benefit from the ideas and experience of the area superintendent. To satisfy this planning responsibility, principals will need the help of the area superintendent's staff. These staff members must be able to help principals identify the needs and attitudes of the people the school serves and plan for the services that centralized departments can provide.

This planning process already occurs informally in many instances, but an increasingly decentralized organization will need systematic, measurable planning to preserve accountability. Building principals must become free to exercise the creativity and judgment their professional training and experience has provided; they should not be burdened with more paper work.

Staffing

Area superintendents will need additional staff to carry out programs with principals and the schools they supervise. Two assistants at the level of pay of an assistant principal are needed.

One assistant should be responsible for program planning. This assistant should be an experienced and creative teacher who could work with building principals and master teachers. The other assistant should concentrate on community relations. He would work with area-wide community groups and help principals improve programs by working with local groups and concerned parents. This assistant should be either a teacher who has been unusually successful in working with the community or a noneducator who has been unusually successful in working with the schools.

Many staff now in the central office in curriculum and staff development should be assigned to the area offices.

The area superintendent should continue to work closely with principals, teachers, and the community to assure his effectiveness in policy-making. Providing assistants should not force the area superintendent into a strictly managerial role.

Any ancillary duties area superintendents now perform which serve primarily system-wide needs rather than area needs should be reassigned to someone with system-wide responsibilities.

The area superintendent already has a tremendously demanding job, and these recommendations broaden his responsibilities. Arrangements must be made in each area to have a responsible person on call at all times should a crisis arise. The area superintendent's office should be open for a greater portion of the day than it is now.

The ideal area superintendent should be well acquainted with his area, yet sensitive enough to its needs that they do not come to seem routine. For this reason, renewal of an area superintendent's six-year term should be contingent upon a thorough evaluation in which his superiors, his subordinates in the school department, and community representatives would participate.

These suggestions provide a blueprint for continued development along the lines established for the Boston schools in 1966. To date, area superintendents have served well; they have proven essential as integrators and *ad hoc* problem-solvers. But as the schools enter the seventies under the penetrating eye of a watchful and often critical clientele, the area superintendents must act with and through their principals to devise the varied programs which children in their areas require. To avoid chaos the school system must institute explicit, systematic program planning at every level. By encouraging diversity and maintaining accountability, the area superintendent becomes a key figure in the administrative process.

Summary

The area superintendents must be educational leaders and planners. Their responsibilities include:

- Participating in the central policy-making, goal-setting process for the entire system
- Developing detailed educational plans for their areas, consistent with the system's goals
- Conducting regular planning meetings with their principals to discuss and resolve area problems and to develop closer communication among the schools in each area
- Reviewing individual building program plans with each principal

Each area superintendent should have two assistants at the pay level of a vice-principal: one assistant for program planning and one assistant for community relations. Also, any special duties, which concern system-wide rather than area needs, should be reassigned to someone with system-wide responsibilities. Meanwhile, specialists concerned with staff development and curriculum should be assigned to work with schools under the area superintendent.

A New Role for Boston's Principals:
Educational and Community Leadership

The demands of urban life and urban education require principals who are educational and community leaders—men and women who are respected by their staffs for their expertise, who take an active role in program development, and who work closely with the community in improving schools and solving community problems. Too often in Boston, as well as in other communities, the principal is an office-based administrator who channels directives from his superiors to his subordinates. Apparently with each passing year and new contract, Boston's principals are forced further from the position of leader. THE PRINCIPAL'S HANDBOOK of the Boston Public Elementary Schools describes the principal's basic role as that of "the representative of the Superintendent of Schools . . . the executive charged with the responsibility of carrying out . . . directives." This is too narrow and restrictive a mandate.

Principals are part of a hierarchical chain of command: the superintendent is at the apex, followed by associates, assistants, department heads, principals, and teachers. The nature of the existing hierarchy makes it difficult for information to flow up as well as down the line. Thus the system places little value on program evaluation and feedback, basic components in an effective organization.

The Boston School Department has required its principals to be functionaries. Its demands on them have been uniform—to carry out system-wide policies and directives. The directives have also tended to be uniform and have not considered the special needs and diverse problems of particular areas. Experienced teachers with the required tenure and additional training become "Boston Principals," considered eligible for assignment to any Boston school rather than for assignments in particular neighborhoods or buildings according to their special backgrounds and talents.

System personnel procedures must change so that the training, skills, and experience of school principals match the area they will serve. Moreover, Boston's principals *must* be given increased authority, resources, and responsibility.

During interviews, parents, teachers, and principals commented on the principal's role. Teachers tend to find that principals do not provide educational leadership. Several principals complained that they are forced to leave the classroom, to ignore parents and community, and to fill out and administer forms.

Several factors may account for principal's tendency to administer rather than lead. Because each addition of a new central department—the system has the tendency to add new departments in response to crises—increases paperwork, the time available to principals for effective leadership decreases. Perhaps tense school-community relations make office work seem more attractive. Features in the union contract and the decrease in age of Boston's teachers may diminish the principal's compatibility with his teachers and in some cases may reduce his capacity to lead. Whatever other specific reasons, the demand for increased paperwork is a serious problem. And today, when a principal's leadership is most crucial to schools and communities, the functionary role in which the principal finds himself is a more critical drawback than ever before.

Requisites for Leadership

The principal's authority must come from two sources: from his personal qualities and from his insistence that freedom and responsibility are built into his role. The strongest basis for authority is one of expertise. If a principal is to lead in the Boston School Department, his power must be based firmly on his expertise, not on formally allocated power.

There are several ways for a principal to develop the necessary respect. First, a principal should have expertise superior to that of a teacher. Principals should know more about teachers, about evaluation, and about their communities. They should have more formal credentials than the teachers they lead. Principals should be chosen after they have advanced training in program development, teacher supervision, evaluation, and community relations, with a training period that includes service in a community agency or on the staff of an area superintendent.

Second, parents and children must be able to identify with their principals. All parties must be willing to communicate with each other. Lack of communication is a frequent criticism of Boston's principals. Assigning Black principals to Black neighborhoods can also further identification, for it can help foster the trust vital to effective leadership.

Third, principals can encourage respect for themselves by respecting others. They can demonstrate their sensitivity and respect toward others by encouraging the people in their areas to participate in decision-making for the school and neighborhood. Parent-teacher advisory councils, recommended elsewhere in this report, provide opportunities for parents, teachers and students to participate in school decisions. If these groups are instrumental in selecting a principal for their area, they are more apt to accept his leadership.

Recommendations

An effective principal for the 1970s must take an active role in program development, personnel development, and community development.

First, the principal should be a team leader in developing educational programs for his school. He should modify system and area curricula to make them suitable for his school. He should guide his teachers in developing new curricula specifically for his school. He should help develop new programs from outside sources, such as museums, and community agencies. And he should provide feedback to area offices and central departments on system-wide programs, for his feedback is necessary for effective planning and evaluation.

Second, he must help his teachers improve their teaching methods and encourage their personal and professional development. He should encourage experienced teachers to keep abreast of new educational trends through school department programs and graduate courses. He should also participate in workshops and courses and keep up with current educational literature.

Third, he must work closely with the people in his community. The principal must do more than respond to criticisms. Rather, he should meet with community groups to help them plan education-related programs. He should attend community meetings, as do many principals, to learn more about the community and to be a representative of his school. A good principal should encourage the school staff to visit students' homes.

Currently, a Boston principal must spend most of his working day solving immediate problems and contending with crises. A principal in an elementary school district is expected to supervise teachers in three or four buildings with as many as 1800 or 2000 children. Yet in Boston, a principal receives only part-time assistance from teaching vice-principals. In other cities and suburbs, an assistant principal works full time on administrative matters.

As of 1970, Boston employed 229 elementary vice-principals; all but eleven are essentially full-time teachers. In elementary school districts, a teaching vice-principal is often placed in charge of a satellite building. He or she must handle emergencies, cope with problems other teachers cannot manage, screen callers to the school, and answer a telephone placed in the vice-principal's classroom. The phone may ring from five to fifteen times a day with parent complaints, requests for assistance, and other matters which are routine in school operation but which conflict directly with the vice-principal's instructional program. Children in these classes are shortchanged educationally. Elsewhere in the Commonwealth, school buildings with 500 or 750 pupils usually have a secretary, and one or two administrators.

Boston's principals and their assistants need opportunities to confer with principals, supervisors, and curriculum development staff in other parts of the state and nation. The current out-of-state travel and convention budget of

$40,000 a year, set by statute for Boston only, is less than the amount budgeted by several nearby communities with one-tenth of Boston's school population. Only one or two of thirty secondary school principals in Boston can attend the National Association of Secondary School Principals meeting each year. A Boston principal would be fortunate to go once in twenty years. Boston school leaders must again develop a national perspective and participate in national conferences on education as do school committee members, the superintendent, and many directors. The statutory limit has the negative effect of keeping many school children away from the sources of new ideas. If a limit is necessary—and this is doubtful—then the guideline should not be a flat rate but a percentage, such as one-tenth of 1 percent of the total budget (e.g., $83,000 in 1970). New principals as well as experienced administrators should be able to attend state, regional, and national meetings. Those who attend must present to their colleagues the ideas, trends, and developments discussed during these conferences.

Schools of education in the Boston area give vouchers (coupons redeemable for courses) to teachers who supervise student teachers and interns, but they do not give them to administrators who may accept from ten to forty student teachers a year. Universities must extend these opportunities to urban school administrators, the best of whom should join the higher education faculties as part-time adjunct professors, clinical professors, and lecturers.

Resources

Adequate resources are essential if Boston's principals are to be leaders. The study staff recommends the following changes:

- The principal should be given a full-time administrative assistant for every 600 pupils in his school community. This person should be a full-time administrator, not a teacher.
  1. Assigning work to assistants should be flexible and at the principal's request in areas such as discipline, scheduling, community liaison work, and observation of beginning staff.
  2. The principal should select this administrator from qualified personnel after personal interviews and a pretraining period which should include pairing experienced administrative assistants with beginners for observation.
- Each satellite elementary building of more than six classrooms should be staffed by a school clerk-receptionist who would handle clerical work and all building needs (supplies, etc.) and act as a receptionist. This person should have business training. An additional Spanish-speaking clerk should serve as registrar and interpreter in each elementary district in which there are at least twenty Spanish-speaking families.

- Time should be set aside during the school year for team building and staff preparation for the following year. All principals, administrative assistants and school secretaries should be employed and paid for twelve months with four weeks vacation.
- Monthly professional meetings should be continued not only among principals in a particular geographic area but also among those at the same educational level in the urban area and its environs. These meetings should coordinate efforts and communicate to the central office staff ideas which concern principals and school staffs. Principals should participate in developing the agenda for these meetings.
- A bill should be introduced into the state legislature to remove the limit on or substantially increase the amount the school department may allocate for professional conferences, especially conferences for principals, supervisors, and assistants. Opportunities to attend conferences should be weighted in favor of personnel in school districts most immediately influenced by change.

The Teacher

The teachers in the Boston school system are great sources of new ideas, activities, programs, and attitudes. Teachers, more than any other group in the system, most often demand change. Of the Boston teachers interviewed, about 36 percent seek major changes in the system (e.g., decentralization of administration); 48 percent show no clear pattern for desired changes; 16 percent seek conservative or reactionary changes (e.g., limiting IPP). A relatively small percentage of teachers suggest no changes for their school or for the system as a whole. Only a few teachers (but several assistant principals) agreed with the teacher who, when asked what he would change in the school system, responded; "I never thought about that. I wish you gave me some time to think about that before you asked it. Offhand, I'd say nothing." Teachers were more apt to make statements like the Roxbury teacher who said; "We need more Black teachers and more specialists concerned with Black problems like Elma Lewis School personnel; basically we need a more decentralized system." Younger teachers and teachers whose experience has not been limited to Boston schools are often the most innovative and most responsive to change.

Encouraging Boston Teachers to Adopt and
Adapt to New Methods and Teaching Styles

A three-sided effort is needed to allow and encourage Boston teachers to adopt and adapt to new teaching methods.

Exposure to New Ideas. *Recruitment.* Before they can adopt new ideas, teachers must first be exposed to them. Boston has succeeded recently in hiring enthusiastic young teachers from all around the United States. These young teachers have varied backgrounds and degrees in many fields.

Model Schools and Training Centers. Model elementary and secondary schools should be established in each of the six school areas. These schools should be open continuously for teacher observations, and teachers should be given two days a year to visit model schools. The staffs of the model schools should give lectures and demonstrations on new techniques several times a year at other schools in their districts.

Training centers should be established with the model schools. Teachers would attend the centers regularly during their tenure and would receive credit towards advanced salary steps. Students, teachers, parents, and other concerned and creative people should be encouraged to present innovative ideas and programs for the model schools. The model schools and training centers should be run by the Department of Staff and Organizational Development in close cooperation with the area superintendents.

Teacher Exchanges. Programs of intra- and inter-city teacher exchanges should be continued and expanded. Teachers should be paid for exchange visits. They should also share and present their observations with their colleagues at workshops and meetings.

Resources. Exposure to new ideas will not, by itself, produce change. Teachers must also be given the resources with which to change. Boston's teachers need:

- Money to work in groups or as individuals to plan and carry out new programs. An initial budget of $100,000 per area should be distributed as grants to individual teachers or groups of teachers who present valid innovative plans.
- Resource centers in each model school to hold materials for new and promising programs and supplementary materials for existing programs.
- Immediate changes in existing physical plant, to allow for greater flexibility and team teaching. Knocking down walls and detaching fixed desks is less expensive than constructing new buildings. The mayor should help the school committee obtain $1,000,000 in state and local funds immediately to carry out these needed alterations.
- A role in establishing the criteria for selection of principals at their schools. Because teachers know their school, their students and their parents, they can give valuable suggestions on what skills and ideas a principal will need.

Encouragement and Accountability. In many ways, teachers are too closely supervised. Teachers in many schools must submit dated and detailed lesson plans each week. For example, some teachers are expected to outline and follow a minute by minute daily schedule. Some criteria set for teachers are inappropriate, e.g., keep noise down, get children to form a straight line, do not allow anyone out of the room.

Teacher evaluation must become more professional and sophisticated.

- An instructional team of several teachers within a school should plan and supervise instruction. Daily schedules and lesson plans should be treated as personal instruments for the teacher rather than as checklists for the supervisor or principal.
- The master teacher and principal should review each teacher's performance annually. This review should be based on classroom visits and demonstrations. Union representatives and school officials should develop standards of accountability such as those now being developed in New York City and elsewhere.

Professionalization through Specialization

For the past few years, the Boston School Department has been moving towards increased teacher specialization. Vestiges of the uniform teaching role remain— all Boston elementary teachers take the same type of exam and most are assigned arbitrarily to schools regardless of the different talents they may possess or the special needs a particular school may have. Boston must begin to acknowledge the diversity not only of its students but also of its teachers. Differentiation of teaching roles, begun with lunch aides and counselors, must spread to new areas. The teaching role must be differentiated by position, subject area, location and time.

Differentiated Positions. As many as 200 Boston teachers should be recognized as leaders in their fields and given extra responsibility for teacher training, team leadership, program development, and community work. They should be paid as much as a principal or director on a twelve-month basis. These teachers would visit and evaluate other teachers and head teacher teams at model schools and training centers.

At the same time, new teachers should enter the system as interns or beginners under the team supervision of other teachers and career leaders. Dozens of others without degrees could begin as teacher aides, study at area colleges part-time, and eventually become teacher interns and assistant teachers. The career ladder would be:

- Teacher aides—community people and others helping students and teachers
- Teachers interns—teachers in training with some teaching responsibility
- Assistant teachers—teachers in their first five years of service working on a team with other teachers, counselors, and aides
- Teachers—teachers of individual classes (e.g., some special classes)—similar to a present teacher
- Team leaders—master or career teachers with extra responsibility for programs and teacher supervision

Teaching Areas. In each of the five positions, subject or teaching specialty areas should be defined, even at the elementary level. Some children would need the same teacher for most of the day; others would profit from the skills and variety of as many as six or eight instructors.

Teaching Location. No teacher can function equally well in every teaching location. Roxbury will seek teachers different from those in Hyde Park-Roslindale. A teacher who has great rapport with students and parents in East Boston may be at a loss in West Roxbury. Every effort must be made to place teachers where talents and abilities will be most useful. This means that teacher candidates must be encouraged to visit the schools, the teachers and principals with whom they might work. Informally, student teachers do this, but so should all other teaching candidates.

Teaching Time. The concepts of the "school day" and "school year" must be expanded beyond 8 A.M. to 3 P.M. and one hundred eighty days. Part-time aides and teachers working on alternative shifts could extend education to extra classes and activities which now cannot fit into the schedule. If timing were more flexible, schools would be able to release students at midday once a week and schedule parent conferences, community agency meetings, and teacher planning sessions. City recreation and other agencies would offer alternative opportunities for children on those afternoons. It is a great waste for schools to be unused on evenings, weekends, and during the summer. School-community cooperation means that communities can benefit by using school buildings, as schools benefit from using community resources.

Teacher Orientation

In the past, "teacher orientation" in Boston has meant a meeting held one day before the opening of school in September. Most new teachers have never visited the schools to which they are assigned, nor met their principals or their future colleagues. A program of teacher orientation should fulfill the following:

- It should introduce the new teacher to the goals and aims of the system at large.
- It should present to the new teacher the aims of the particular school in which he or she will teach.
- It should acquaint the teacher with the environment of that school—other schools, special services, boundaries, libraries, churches, health facilities, youth centers, and businesses. It should give the teacher an opportunity to familiarize himself with the physical plant and the materials he will use during the school year.
- It should provide an opportunity for the new teacher to meet the staff of the school and other new teachers in the district and system.

New teachers also need time to prepare their classrooms and instructional materials. To provide true orientation, a program requires more than one day. Many systems have orientation programs which last one week or longer. Social functions, an introduction to professional, service, and other school groups, and visits to community resources should also be scheduled in the orientation program.

Team leaders and other experienced teachers should be present during orientation, and efforts should be made to pair new teachers with experienced teachers. The new teacher—a novice, or new to Boston, or merely new to the particular school—should be made to feel a part of the school team and his or her role should be carefully outlined. The teaching contract should include a provision for a longer orientation period.

Functions of the Central Departments

Some critics of the school system believe that little or no central staff is necessary, that schools can run themselves. They seem to forget it is necessary to recruit teachers, order supplies and conduct the business of a system, plan for new buildings, and provide a variety of special services.

Actually much of what is now done centrally could be done by individual schools or by areas. Teachers need guidance and assistance at the classroom or school level. Curricula and materials could be selected or adapted at the school and classroom level. Many pupil services should be coordinated at the school or area level. Even some repair and maintenance work could be directed from the area level.

The responsibilities of the central staff of the Boston School Department should include:

- Recruiting all personnel and with principals, teachers, and other staff participating in the selection of staff according to the needs of each school
- Developing an overall program in basic skills but with considerable options at each school about implementation, variations, materials, and alternatives (e.g., "grade level" curriculum guides are considered less useful by teachers today than outlines of sequence and scope of skills with an evaluation of various related materials)
- Preparing a budget that provides a plan for a system, an area, and a school, one that displays alternative programs with estimated costs and benefits
- Furnishing books, supplies, media, and other resources used in instructional program
- Planning buildings and coordinating affiliations with other agencies for educational projects
- Arranging classes for special students—the bilingual, the talented, the re-

tarded, the handicapped, the disturbed, and the unusually motivated—and testing, counseling, and providing physical and mental health services for all students

- Coordinating vocational-technical-occupational education for all students

- Handling employee negotiations, payrolls, accounts and audits, and other business support services including food, transportation, and major repairs.

A school system needs planning not only for facilities but planning for its own renewal, for constant shifts in the organization of its services, and for periodic retraining and upgrading of its staff. Planning requires a substantial system capacity to evaluate the worth and impact of programs and to analyze data to understand changes that may be necessary.

This report offers specific suggestions for strengthening the system's planning and evaluation capacities and for reducing the role of the centralized, somewhat distant, school department. The central office should provide services and help assess the results of education, not try to restrict, a process which must be changeable, human, and dynamic.

Functions of the School Committee

Traditionally, the school committee is the policy-maker for a local educational agency. In practice, the Boston School Committee spends an inordinate amount of time making very specific personnel appointments, assignments, transfers, and taking other specific actions. Its members are expected to review and pass on the value of every text. The committee must also grant hearings to local groups and serve as the final board to review personnel grievances—another personnel function, not a policy role. Decisions made during the period October 1967 to June 1969 fall into these categories.

Instead of concentrating on personnel matters, the Boston School Committee should use most of its energy in deciding educational policy questions: the value of existing programs, the priorities of programs, expansion, relationships with other agencies, and the search for new ways to make education productive. The budget cycle provides one opportunity over a period of several months for review of alternate programs with staff-prepared analyses of each program.

Most of the personnel functions, except the appointment of a superintendent, can be delegated to personnel officials. This is especially true of transfers and nonacademic appointments.

Area superintendents should handle the hearing function, with the help of area councils of parents selected from each neighborhood and school. A city-wide school committee should rarely take two or three hours on problems that could be solved nearer the level of the school. Nor should citizen and parent groups wait three to six months for a place on the hearing agenda.

The second major function of the school committee should be to evaluate the work of the school system and make recommendations concerning the extra resources needed to help certain schools and students perform more successfully. The committee must have more information on successful programs and problem areas. As much as one-third of the meeting time should be spent reviewing reports on the performance of children, school staffs, and regular and special programs.

These changes require holding members of the staff accountable to the citizens through the elected board. Therefore, a committee cannot play favorites. Nor can committee members expect staff members to purchase tickets to annual testimonial dinners or parties, a practice which substitutes loyalty for performance, gratitude for results. School employees need a municipal Hatch Act to protect them from political obligations. The side-effects of past mixing of political and professional activity include public loss of confidence in the school committee and an increase of cynicism by school employees on how to get ahead in the system and on how to get salary raises.

Yet a school committee member incurs expenses. Later in the report a specific proposal provides for minimum compensation, and, for most of the committee, a reduction in the campaign costs and support needed for election. Taking politics out of the schools was a goal of urban school reformers early in this century. The price was high in the loss of citizen participation.

School-Community Relations

Community relations cannot be improved without frank recognition that the problems of the past few years are based partly on the failure of school people and parents to listen to each another. This failure is a reflection of communication problems within the system itself.

A 1970 report by the Education Planning Center of the Boston School Department recommends that communication be improved by changes at the local level—commitment by local administrators to active roles in community affairs, the formation of local school task forces, the use of nonprofessional staff from the local communities, and the formation of advisory councils.

Unfortunately, the school department often tends to downgrade communication from parents. Parents are low in power, information, and authority, and their critical remarks about the schools or about individual teachers are often considered to be based on inadequate knowledge and faulty judgment, and, therefore, do not present a challenge that requires action. Real communication requires an equal balance of power, information, and authority. If community relations are to become more than the school department's public relations, parents must work to increase their influence.

By organizing, parents have attempted to equalize their power with that of school administrators. By conducting research and seeking allies in the universities and the suburbs, they have attempted to gather enough information to be able to seek specific changes. By seeking training, attending conferences, and even conducting their own educational programs, they have increased their authority to make judgments about education. The number of parents seeking to make themselves heard is increasing; they are beginning to establish two-way communication with the school department.

Unfortunately, many school department personnel seem to feel that responding to parents' criticisms and suggestions would threaten the educational program of the schools and their own positions. In a number of local situations a principal has refused to meet with organized groups of parents, insisting that he was willing to talk with *individual* parents at any time.

This prohibition against organized parent groups can be carried to absurd lengths. When the leaders of the Home and School Associations in one part of Boston formed a coordinating council to work for some moderate goals, they were told by personnel "downtown" that they could not use Home and School in connection with their efforts.

In another neighborhood parents tried to bridge the racial gap dividing the

43

parents of a predominantly black school from those of a predominantly white school in the same elementary district by electing co-presidents of the Home and School—one white, one black. "Downtown" informed them that only one could be president. The black parent agreed to become vice-president—but many other black parents felt betrayed and the ability of the local Home and School to solve a community problem was destroyed.

The effect of this resistance to independent parents' organizations is to insist that those parents who wish to communicate with school officials, offer suggestions, make requests or express their educational priorities, must always do so from a weak position.

School personnel have also prevented parents from acquiring information about schools and programs which parents need to communicate their concerns and priorities. Statistics on student performance are not released in an aggregated form, which makes it impossible for parents to judge, for example, whether their own children have individual problems or share in a pattern of failure. Ill-informed parents will often choose the worst possible interpretation of the clues they receive about the schools. By concealing failure, schools often simultaneously prevent recognition of success. Several principals noted their frustration when, after substantial improvements had been made in their schools, parents continued to judge schools as if no change had occurred.

Some administrators and teachers, particularly in low-income neighborhoods, are unwilling to give parents an opportunity to become familiar with the process of schooling. Few parents interviewed had ever observed an ordinary class session, and in at least one case, development of a library program had a great impact on a group of parents because it gave them their first chance to see the ordinary routine of a school. Some principals are willing to accept nonprofessional volunteers only if they are *not* from the neighborhood of the school.

Principals have some reason for their caution, for the results of parental involvement have sometimes been unfortunate. However, the failure of some attempts can be explained by inadequate planning and execution. If an organized community group becomes hostile, it is often because school representatives were evasive, or because the group was not given opportunities to feel a sense of accomplishment.

Parents do not always have a good enough understanding of the limitations under which school personnel have to operate. Greater openness about these limitations would be a valuable form of communication between the school and the home. But parents also have a right to expect that school personnel will recognize the difficulties inherent in creating and maintaining an organization of parents, and the need of these organizations to point to accomplishments. Too often an organization will work for months to persuade the school department to meet some local need, only to be denied all credit when the need is met. It is common for administrators to feel that they should not acknowledge having responded to community pressure.

Too often, parents are not given realistic alternatives from which to choose. Usually, the only choice is whether or not to adopt or continue a given program. Outside consultants working with community groups could help generate other alternatives. However, the school staff is generally hostile to "outsiders." In several sections of Boston, school staff members felt that APACs (Area Planning Action Council—the local antipoverty agencies) had deliberately tried to turn parents against the schools.

Despite the difficulties outside consultants may cause, parents have a legitimate need for independent advice on educational matters. To some extent the Educational Planning Center can provide advice to parent groups. However, the EPC is not prepared to help parents form critical judgments of the effectiveness of their local schools. Thus parents still need advice from independent consultants.

There are advantages and disadvantages in allowing community-based agencies like APACs and the Model Neighborhood Boards to serve as consultants. These agencies are committed to the particular communities where they operate and are fully independent of school department influence. At the same time, they need to generate widespread community support to ensure their survival and thus, often seek to overcome apathy by making dramatic charges against the schools. This approach does not encourage joint problem-solving by local school staff and parents. What is needed is a separation between the frankly political function of creating demand for major reforms in the educational system and the consultant's function of helping community groups learn about their local schools. The Model Cities Administration has already developed a program of technical assistance to parent groups involved in new school planning and in program planning.

Parents must be organized if they are to communicate with school staff, and they must have access to information and expertise. However, communication will fail if the principals, the area superintendents, and the teachers are not seriously committed to the idea. Teachers and principals who are willing to communicate with parents must be highly rewarded in the rating process. At present, school personnel draw as little attention as possible to their relationships with groups critical of any aspect of the schools—even the physical condition of school buildings! Many teachers and administrators nevertheless are committed to work quietly with such groups.

When the school department revises the rating process, commitment to parent-school communication should receive increased weight. Parents should be involved in this rating process, since only they are in a position to judge whether school staff are truly helpful and responsive. The program developed in Minneapolis-St. Paul to evaluate high schools on a regular, ongoing basis, involving students and parents in the process, could be valuable in both elementary and secondary schools in Boston. One virtue of this approach is that it does not attempt to judge individual staff members but the entire local school.

It thereby provides a context within which to recognize excellence in any staff members—including excellence in communicating with parents—and to reward it.

Recommendations

School-community relations are a responsibility of every member of the School Department Staff; it is especially the responsibility of those at the school and area levels. It would be inappropriate to assign this work to a central unit in the School Department. Additional administrative staff at the school and area levels would free principals and teachers to interact with parents and community groups.

Staff members should be rewarded for effort and expertise in school-community relations; such effort should influence appointment to administrative positions.

- The school department must assign primary responsibility for community relations to the area superintendent, principals, and teachers.
- All school staff (e.g., secretaries, area superintendents' staff) who come in contact with the community should receive additional human relations training. They should also be rewarded for excellent performance in community relations.
- The school system should expand the use of volunteers and paid aides as part of the school-community program.
- The school department should expand efforts with the Park and Recreation Department and other agencies to make school facilities available to community groups.
- School councils, such as the one now operating at the Lewenberg School, should be formed for all schools so that parents can participate more constructively in the education of their children.
- The school committee should be restructured to give equal representation to each section of the city.

Parent Involvement—Volunteers and Aides

Some parents in Boston take an active role in Home and School, but Home and School activity is generally peripheral to what goes on in the school. The energies of active, concerned parents are not being directed into the learning process, but into raising funds and presenting informational programs. Parents are taking the initiative in demanding physical improvements in several Boston schools but in most schools involvement of parents in *educational* matters is slight.

The School Volunteers for Boston have had some success in involving neighborhood residents in their programs, but relatively few Boston parents are actually working in classrooms and with children. Significantly, some principals resisted accepting neighborhood residents as nonpaid aides but welcomed volunteers from the suburbs.

Some parents and neighborhood residents have been employed in connection with federally-funded programs directed at schools in low-income areas—but in small numbers with limited autonomy. More than one-thousand neighborhood residents are currently employed as school lunch aides, working for three hours a day at $2.35 an hour to relieve teachers during lunch period. Generally, these aides have not been asked to assume responsibilities beyond supervising the children to assure an orderly lunch period.

Several hundred neighborhood residents are working as library aides in a program developed by the School Volunteers for Boston. This program is in some respects a model for parental involvement in the educational process, because it involves direct contact with children in a learning situation, and provides a service otherwise not available.

Most parents in Boston are not really involved in the education process at this time. This lack of involvement is unfortunate at a time when demands are being made upon the school system to meet new needs, or to meet old needs with new standards of service. It is also unfortunate because educational research reveals the crucial role of parents in guiding children toward scholastic success or failure.

Parents can assist with certain aspects of the instructional process. As teachers develop increasingly specialized skills, it becomes more and more appropriate for them to concentrate on those aspects of teaching which demand their professional training. The heart of any profession is diagnosis and prescription, and there is a growing tendency in every branch of the human services to assign much of the treatment responsibility to technicians and auxiliary workers who have not had as much specialized training.

Teachers are gradually discovering that aides can actually help with some of the instruction. Parents working in classrooms may supervise individual work assigned by the teacher, or present material to the entire class, while the teacher observes the children's responses. This classroom arrangement could be part of a comprehensive reorganization of instruction, including team teaching, greater use of resource centers and partnership schools like those proposed by Model Cities.

In this way the professional skills of the teacher are emphasized and the amount of adult time and help which each child receives is increased. It becomes possible to answer questions when they arise, to praise accomplishments as they occur, to give careful attention to what children are saying and to respond carefully, and to handle disciplinary problems with the care they deserve.

Second, parents can help overcome language and other barriers between the school and the child. Ethnic, racial, and language barriers to learning are complex and often frustrating to teachers and principals. Parents could help teachers recognize the influence of their students' home environment and therefore, understand their problems.

If the schools are to respect diversity, teachers must understand the values of the many groups in the urban community. A parent who is working sympathetically with the teacher could help a great deal.

At the same time, parents working in the classroom could provide positive adult models, thereby relieving children of the notion that foreign birth or dark skin means low status. This will succeed only when parents are working in responsible and significant roles. The parent who does only menial chores in the classroom may simply reinforce the stereotypes.

Involving low income or minority-group parents in the classroom is no substitute for recruiting minority professional staff, but it will provide an opportunity to obtain some results quickly, and to give children models who are clearly neighborhood-based.

Third, parent involvement captures the energies of the most committed individuals and community leaders for the work of education. The issue today is no longer whether or not parents will criticize schools but whether they will be *informed* and constructive critics, with a good understanding of what school staffs are attempting to do and of the complexity of education. If they are well informed, they may be just as critical, just as insistent that the schools' priorities must be changed, but they will also be helpful and realistic and will not criticize unjustly.

It is very important for school personnel and children that significant numbers of parents have first-hand experience of the instructional process. They can best gain this experience by working closely with teachers and administrators as they respond to daily problems. This is even more vital as the number of parent councils increases.

The Success of Mixed Staffing

Throughout the country, one classroom teacher in four now has the support of a nonprofessional aide. Over one-thousand aides are employed in one capacity or another in the Boston schools, but many of these replace teachers at noon and do not really work directly with the teacher or aid in instruction.

Generally, the use of aides in education has not been as innovative as their use in nursing, mental health, addiction programs, correctional facilities and social work. Schools have been slower to recognize the importance of giving real responsibility to community people. Educational leaders have not yet found ways to use the special talents and insights of "community staff."

One of the problems in using community staff is financial. If they are to feel fully committed, they must be paid adequately on an annual contract not an hourly wage. The Boston School Department must make a more determined effort to use federal and state funds to train and employ community staff. The department should not overlook funding through programs normally considered "manpower" or "income maintenance." Boston should continue to bid for programs like the Careers Opportunity Program, which provides for training and some supervision of new careerists for the schools.

A second difficulty arises because school staffing has remained so remarkably stable for three generations. Too often, teachers and administrators may treat community staff as additional school secretaries or clerks, not as members of a new educational team.

A third difficulty is that parents tend to have their own ideas of what school is about, based on their childhood experiences in school. Most parents have not been exposed to new thinking about education. In one Boston classroom, for example, the teacher allowed children to play records and move about the classroom during their lunch period. As soon as she left the room, however, the parent aide made the children shut off the record, return to their seats and eat their lunch in silence. Paradoxically, the more progressive teachers, who strongly believe in community involvement in education, may also find it most difficult to work with parents in the school. Both teachers and aides may need team teaching orientation sessions to arrive at mutual understanding; otherwise, each may become critical of the other's work style.

Teachers and administrators in some schools in low-income neighborhoods are opposed to involving parents in teaching situations because they feel parents represent qualities from which children must be rescued. If black children are considered culturally deprived because of their backgrounds, it is difficult to understand how their parents can be a valuable part of their educations.

If, on the other hand, schools have a responsibility to help children value and strengthen their ethnic origins, then it is important that adults who feel comfortable with their own ethnic values and behavior patterns be in responsible positions in the schools, side by side with other adults who represent different behavior patterns and values.

Unfortunately parents who are active in school affairs often report that they are made to feel that their activity is significant only as it supports the work of teachers and other professional staff. They are not allowed to feel that they are indispensable members of the school team.

The Boston School Department can and must find ways to make effective use of the energy, commitment, skills and insights of all parents, including those in low-income neighborhoods and members of minority groups.

Recommendations

- Community staff members, aides and volunteers, must be made a regular part of the staffing pattern of the school department. They should be treated like other educational staff, and be placed organizationally under the associate superintendent for personnel, not under the secretary of the school committee (as lunch aides are) or any department.

- Community staff should be employed on a regular annual contract, subject to a probationary period. They should enjoy the same protection of due process as other teaching staff.
- Implementation of mixed staffing at a school should be conditional on the development of a plan by the principal, teachers, and parents, with the assistance of whatever consultant help they might request from the school department or from other agencies. This plan should describe the responsibilities of community staff, and how the role of professional teachers and other staff would be redefined. It should include procedures for recruiting, screening, training, and supervising the community staff.
- This plan should then be reviewed and accepted at the area level by a board which includes administrators, teachers, and parents. This board should have one full-time staff member, the Coordinator of Community Staff, to assist in reviewing and evaluating plans. The Board should work with principals, supervisors, and community staff as they carry out approved plans.
- An additional assistant principal at each school or elementary district should help develop an approved plan for community staff and supervise the work of the community staff. These positions should be filled by individuals who have demonstrated their rapport with parents and their skill in educational innovation.
- The school department's staff development and in-service training programs should include community staff. Community staff should have every opportunity to become qualified as teachers or administrators if they wish to do so.
- The School Volunteers for Boston should continue to play a significant part in developing new approaches to using nonprofessional staff in educational roles. The primary function of the School Volunteers for Boston should be to innovate, taking advantage of their organizational flexibility and the low commitment of school department resources required for their programs.

Parent and Community Councils

Boston once involved citizens in the management of the schools in each ward. Today, thousands of citizens participate in meetings of the Boston Home and School Association, an organization which is supported by the school department. The school department provides office space and salary for a staff coordinator for the Home and School.

Many parents throughout the city felt the Home and School Association and its executive board of parents and staff members provided for adequate parent participation. Others complained about educator domination, meaningless activities, and the scheduling of Home and School meetings at times when parents cannot attend. Boston staff members admitted that building principals often select and assign teacher members to the association board.

Recently, Boston parents have developed several alternatives to the Home and School Association. The Friends of the Mackey School suggest new programs, fight for more resources, and arrange for volunteers at this South End school. After a crisis, the Solomon Lewenberg School Council created an advisory board; the board at this junior high school consists of elected parents, teachers, hired aides and students who have helped develop community support. The King-Timilty Council resulted from school department, parent, and university concern about the two junior high schools and the eleven feeder elementary schools. Another six or seven schools sponsor local parent associations or councils.

The Lewenberg and Mackey groups fight for extra resources. The Boston School Department was awarded a three year grant of $500,000 each year for the King-Timilty Council. This grant pays for additional staff, compensation to council members for time spent in meetings, and curriculum and materials development.

The school department has learned many lessons—some positive and some negative:

- Parent and community representatives show great concern about a school in a troubled or transitional neighborhood and want to be involved in the search for solutions.
- It is costly and time-consuming to hold school council special elections in which only a small percentage of eligible citizens vote (this was also true of New York City's community board elections in 1970 and of antipoverty and Model Cities board elections throughout most of the United States).
- Local coalitions of parents and educators want action on school problems and, if they are mobilized, they will fight for necessary resources. Teachers or parents, rather than principals, may become leaders and bring about action in support of school programs.
- Parents will meet endlessly—and not always productively—if compensated for their time. But large sums of money will not necessarily solve a school's problems without a concerned principal and a staff which he has helped recruit.
- No council will work, and parent dissatisfaction can actually increase, if the school committee and administrative staff refuse to share their power with concerned parents in a neighborhood. Often, the central body can do little to correct a local situation without parental support.

Critics of urban education do not think advisory councils will work. Many of them advocate either breaking city school systems up into community con-trolled districts or creating alternatives to the public schools (store-front academies, learning centers, free schools, experimental schools). Meanwhile, many city school boards do nothing, hoping that the criticism will die down or that good public relations can soothe the critics.

Discussions and interviews with Boston parents indicate that most feel frustrated but optimistic about the schools. They do not want to disrupt the schools. They want a chance to work with school officials to reduce tensions and resolve controversies peacefully. The council format can offer parents a voice in the schools they support through taxes and their children's participation.

Recommendations

- At the request of ten or more parents in a school, a council should be formed. Councils should consist of all concerned parents and school staff members, and should have an executive board of five parents and three educators.
  1. The parents should be selected by ballot at an annual meeting and school fair or exhibition in June of each year. Parents should be elected as chairman, vice-chairman, secretary, treasurer, and area delegate.
  2. Two teachers should be selected by ballot at an annual meeting of teachers, counselors, and other staff members.
  3. The principal or headmaster should be an ex-officio member of the council.
- Councils should be involved in annual school budget requests, staffing decisions, and building alteration plans. They should develop criteria for the selection of principals and headmasters. They should review, discuss, and make recommendations annually on a school achievement profile prepared by the Department of Research and Evaluation.
- Councils should meet monthly. They should cooperate with other city agencies—e.g., health centers—to develop programs and services for adults and children on a year-round basis. Councils should be encouraged to experiment with new programs, to review grant proposals, to interview potential candidates for the principalship, and to apply for grants and special projects.
- Area councils should consist of one delegate from each school council. They should meet monthly, encourage, help organize and sustain school councils, discuss program staffing and financial needs of schools and neighborhoods in the area, and develop cooperative programs with other agencies, businesses, and community groups. Three principals, three teachers, and three students should also be selected for each area council. The council should select its own chairman and consider the area superintendent to be its executive director and chief of staff. Each area council may need a different combination of staff assistants, e.g., Chinese or Spanish-speaking aides, or reading specialists or experts in programs for the talented. Councils in some areas may often break into work groups for distinct sections of the city, e.g., Charlestown or East Boston.

- Each area council should designate two delegates to a city education council of twelve parent members and six educators, ordinarily including the area superintendent. This council could include teachers, students, and other members when appropriate. This city-wide group should meet periodically with the deputy superintendent for field operations and with the superintendent to discuss the needs of the city, the special needs of each area, and recommendations for change. Every two years this body should prepare a report for the school committee on the three kinds of councils.

What will happen to the Home and School Association? In some cases, Home and School officers might overlap with the council. The association in many neighborhoods would continue to sponsor meetings, concerts, plays, and coffees. However, the advisory council's role should go beyond that of the association; the council can participate more actively in setting school priorities and discussing programs and results.

A School Profile on Problems and Performance

Parents expect full and candid information on their children's talents, accomplishments, problems, and needs. Letter grades, symbols, and stanine scores do not always satisfy them—not when more descriptive measures of achievement can be used (instead of a "*B*" in typing, how many correct words were typed per minute; instead of a mark in reading, an explanation of the level of reading proficiency a child has reached).

Similarly, each year parent groups and school councils should see a "profile" of their school's resources and performance. This profile should include:

- How many teachers are in the school? How many years of experience, in Boston and elsewhere, do they have? How many are new, how many tenured, compared to the system average?
- What special programs are conducted in the school? What aides and extra staff are used?
- Which junior high or high schools have recent graduates attended? What has happened to them (e.g., known dropout rates, college acceptances)?
- What are the test scores for each grade or level, by subject or skill areas? Are there school-wide patterns of success or weakness?
- How much does the school spend on teachers and counselors, custodians, books and materials, repairs and alterations, special staff, and lunches?
- What are projected enrollments for the next three years?

This information should be shared and discussed with parents who can then help develop and support constructive programs of action. Without honest reporting, the school department cannot rely on support from parent groups and school councils.

Student Relations

Support for student participation in educational decision-making has grown over the last ten years. Formerly, the focus has been primarily on college and university campuses, but secondary school students have recently begun expressing their concerns as well.

The responses to student discontent in Boston and elsewhere have included relaxing class and behavior codes, expanding the roles of student councils, granting wider participation in administrative selection activities, and restraining and expelling student advocates. The general results have been to transform a vocal, articulate, committed minority into a powerful bloc, to increase the awareness of the potential power of a large minority of "wait and see" students, and to maximize tension on the part of staff and administration. Generally, individual schools and areas have handled problems effectively, but in some cases, solutions have not come easily.

Against this background the study staff conducted interviews with a number of students from various high schools and junior high schools, visited five schools, attended student discussion sessions (both black and white) and held conversations with staff members at many schools.

Two facts stand out:

- Considerable fragmentation and disunity exists among Boston students. Fragmentation is found among groups as well as within groups and thereby makes it almost impossible to identify any significant city-wide student pressure groups.
- Until the 1970-71 school year, no significant student pressure groups were working to increase or expand the student's role in educational decision-making in Boston.

Rather, students interviewed had a live-it-out-till-graduation or drop out attitude. They were afraid that this report would identify them as individuals and that repercussions would result from their talks with interviewers. They felt that past or future school upheavals would bring about no important changes in their schools. In fact, they felt that nothing could change unless racial, religious, and economic differences were resolved among their classmates, the staff, and the administration. They did not see the Boston schools responding to community pressures other than those pressures for stronger adherence to law and order. They were basically not interested in working for change, not because it was undesirable, but because it was unlikely. Half of those interviewed indicated that they would work for change in other situations—on college campuses, in jobs, or in raising families.

The early 1970s produced a number of incidents in secondary schools where students were vitally involved in resolving crisis situations. In one instance, at one high school a knifing and subsequent racial problems forced closing the school and generated city-wide concern. A council of students was instrumental in calming the situation and in supporting the administration in returning the school to its academic program. Students worked with school officials and the Mayor's Office of Human Rights to solve the immediate crisis. However, when the normal school climate was reestablished, the students' role in problem-solving was discontinued.

A critical situation at a second school involved surface racial tensions and underlying problems concerning administrative policy toward pupils. Before a complete shut-down, a group of students and staff were productively involved in efforts to identify problems so that they might be resolved. The attempt ultimately failed; yet the idea of involving students in the resolution process helped keep a bad situation from becoming worse. Even after the problems of 1969-70, there is no strong student movement for a voice in governing the school.

At a third high school a crisis involving racial tension and damage to the school led to constructive planning of ways to revise the curriculum and change staffing procedure. As a result, damage was kept minimal and disruption was avoided. Students were extremely reticent and so alienated from each other that it was only with great difficulty that they could work together to solve the problems which caused their anger.

Lewenberg Junior High School has had pupils on the Community Advisory Board for some time. But only as Spring began were they participating members, despite their avowed dissatisfaction with the school and the recognition that they are vital to the community board's success.

These events indicate that where crises have existed (or still exist), students provided necessary talent to solve problems. Logically, their talents could be even more useful in preventing crisis situations from developing. In the cases cited, however, students did not exert significant pressure for a decision-making role before a crisis occurred.

In late Spring a student requested that the school committee establish a city-wide student advisory board. His plan was basically for the school committee to recognize a city-wide student council to which individual school councils would send delegates. After some discussion, the school committee granted the request. Membership consists of two members from each high school. One of the two is chosen by the student body—most likely through the building student council; the other is chosen by the administration and staff of the school. The school department included a provision that the city-wide student group should be carefully monitored.

Recommendations for Students

- The school department should plan to involve students in the educational decision-making process on a school-by-school basis. In each school, students who are interested should be given every opportunity to develop leadership skills, group participation skills, and problem analysis and solution skills.

The Educational Planning Center in its work with the cluster concept at the Lewenberg School has demonstrated its ability to help individual schools work with a student group. The EPC should help design ways to involve students in school decision-making.

- Student councils should be encouraged to deal with as many questions as possible to develop student interest in decision-making. They should not be given responsibility for only trivial tasks. Presently individual headmasters determine the qualifications necessary to run for student council. A uniform code of eligibility for serving on student councils should be developed and adopted, with care taken so that the qualifications do not prevent the council from honestly reflecting the composition of a school's population. For example, specific academic requirements may prevent Black and Puerto Rican representation on these councils.
- The school department should inform students about their rights as well as about their responsibilities. Traditionally, students have had no rights to appeal suspension or other disciplinary actions. The Massachusetts Law Reform Institute has compiled a brief pamphlet on student rights which is suitable for distribution in schools. School officials, with the assistance of the Law Department, should continue to clarify a student's right to request a review of possible injustices and to convey student views to school officials appropriately.
- Child labor legislation, which mandates that children must be in school during school hours, must not limit innovation. The success of the work study program in Boston and the parkway program in Philadelphia shows that many students can use their freedom wisely. Students might contract with school officials to work on ecology and city beautification campaigns, in hospitals and museums, and with younger students on tutoring and special help projects.
- Finally, a Boston public high school student should be an official observer and, when it is legal, a full member of the school committee.

Recommendations for Staff

The school department should allow teachers who demonstrate unusual skill in relating to and cooperating with student government to be released from regular classroom teaching duties to work with student organizations and to help other teachers develop the skills, insights, and techniques necessary for healthy teacher-student relations.

School officials must take further steps to encourage teachers to revise curricula and develop new materials. Teachers must be rewarded for efforts to develop meaningful curricular materials and programs.

Recommendations for Administration

Building administrators must be retrained to develop the skills they need to deal effectively with today's students and teachers.

Personnel from the Educational Planning Center and Mayor's Office of Human Rights could assist in this retraining effort.

The school department must give building administrators greater responsibility and accountability for the operation of individual schools to enable them to gain the confidence and trust of students and teachers.

Administrators must become more aware of the necessity for greater student involvement in the operation of the schools. Boston administrators should observe and discuss models for productive, positive student involvement, such as those in Concord or Brookline, or the Lewenberg School Advisory Board.

Racial Imbalance

Clearly any planning for the future must consider the Racial Imbalance Act.

Since 1965 the view of some black leaders about the immediate good of school integration has changed. However, opinion surveys of both white and minority groups in Boston reveal that parents want their children to have quality integrated education. Boston and its suburbs have succeeded in some efforts to reduce imbalance—through METCO (Metropolitan Council for Educational Opportunity), the parent-run EXODUS, open enrollment, and the new Trotter School. Still Boston has more students in racially imbalanced schools in 1973 than it had in 1965.

The Coleman Report indicated that student achievement rises most in schools integrated not only by race but also by social class. This suggests greater emphasis on programs giving students of different races and socioeconomic status the chance to learn together. Some sections of Boston provide both kinds of diversity; many suburbs do also. To insist that every urban neighborhood or working class suburb assists with the Racial Imbalance Law may be a grave mistake.

A Racial Imbalance Task Force of state and Boston officials has met since 1965. This group has reviewed and recommended plans for more than thirty schools, half of the plans contributing directly to the eventual elimination of racial imbalance in Boston and therefore eligible for 65 percent state subsidy. After initial delays, school construction under the Racial Imbalance Act is now comparatively rapid. More new schools have opened between 1967 and 1972 than in the previous ten years.

Community attitudes are often one obstacle to elimination of racial imbalance. Another problem is reliance on the city and state to initiate plans to reduce imbalance. The state and the city still lack aides, incentives, and sufficient staff.

Although the Imbalance Law has been found constitutional, it includes some oversimplified and inequitable provisions. For example, the simple distinction between white and nonwhite blurs over racial distinctions within the latter category. Specifically, the Abraham Lincoln School has at times been one-third white, one-third Black, and one-third Chinese, yet is is classified as 66 percent nonwhite, and racially imbalanced. Furthermore, a deeply-troubled school might be 55 percent low-income Puerto Rican and 45 percent Black, yet under the law it would be considered to have a satisfactory mix. Worst of all, the law has made it difficult to replace old schools in the South End and Roxbury sections until the Trotter and CCED (Committee for Community Educational Development) experiments prove the magnet school concept feasible.

The 50 percent cutoff figure, intended to be an indicator of imbalance but inevitably used as a yardstick for all plans, creates other problems. In 1965 there was no discussion of methods to alleviate imbalance other than the method of avoiding a projected school population of more than 50 percent nonwhite. The act required evaluation by the State Board of Education and the Commissioner of Education which subsequently appeared in a separate study by the Harvard Center for Law and Education.

Meanwhile, the state and Boston should develop proposals that would qualify for federal aid under the education amendments of 1972. One approach which might qualify is the Partnership School Concept offered as a plan to the State Racial Imbalance Task Force.

Additional state and federal resources should support magnet schools, urban-suburban cooperation, partnership plans, and other innovative approaches to reduce racial imbalance in city schools. Boston, with state technical assistance, should apply for federal aid to develop innovative programs to combat racial imbalance on a local and metropolitan basis.

An Ombudsman for the Boston Schools

Complex problems of a large urban school system require resolution in a just, impartial way in a reasonable length of time. Problem-solving methods that now exist in Boston are often too slow and too involved.

An ombudsman for the Boston schools would be an impartial officer appointed to receive, investigate, and expedite solutions to complaints received from individuals. He must be concerned with developing effective procedures, providing adequate and equal treatment to Boston citizens and pinpointing dissatisfaction with the system.

The ombudsman, to be independent and impartial, should *not* be part of the administrative structure of the school department. Instead, he should be appointed by the attorney general of the Commonwealth and paid by the state.

The ombudsman should be able to initiate investigations based on individual complaints, newspaper stories, or any other form of information. He should be free from the considerations that might inhibit the school committee from raising certain issues.

To safeguard his independence, the ombudsman should be removed only after the school committee issues a formal complaint, which is then adjudicated by some outside authority of the calibre of the Supreme Judicial Court of the Commonwealth. This does not mean that the ombudsman should be appointed for life; rather, he should serve a limited term (perhaps four or five years) and not succeed himself.

The qualities essential for the school ombudsman would be the ability to collect and weigh evidence and the ability to assess accurately the claims of aggrieved parents and students.

Rights and Procedures

The ombudsman and his deputies should be empowered to inspect all records and communications of the school department, to call for explanations, and to attend any meetings or department deliberations. He should be able to call hearings that require the presence of any school department employee. He should be able to visit any school without advance notice.

The ombudsman should not have the right to require specific administrative action or reverse any decision. He is not an administrative court, nor has he ultimate responsibility for decision-making. On the other hand, he should not be limited to issuing private "suggestions" to personnel. The ombudsman's rulings should always be made publicly.

Claimants should exhaust all school system remedies before the ombudsman begins an investigation. However, he should be free to undertake an investigation before the usual remedies have been exhausted, if, in his judgment, the complaint concerns an issue that is especially pressing—one that could lead to student or community disorders—or that cannot be settled by the usual procedures. Most important, the office of the Ombudsman should itself be a model of responsive and impartial procedures.

5

School Department Personnel

Six education school deans in the Boston area conducted an intensive study of the school department's rating system.[a] Simultaneously, the Boston School Study group held over fifty interviews on personnel-related issues with employees at all levels of the Boston School Department. This group also conducted a day's personnel workshop and discussion with city teachers and administrators, and examined personnel practices in other educational systems.

These are the major proposals of the deans' study conducted in 1970:

- The Boston Teacher's Examination should be eliminated. The National Teacher's Exam should be the only method used to test teacher applicants, except in subject areas NTE does not cover. To meet this deficiency, the school department should contract with an outside testing agency to compile examinations in these subject areas. Although teaching candidates should still be recruited by the associate superintendent for personnel, applicants should be interviewed by administrators and teachers at individual schools, and the final selection of teachers should be made at the building level.
- To counter the tendency of excellent teachers to become administrators for financial reasons, master teacher positions should be created in numbers equivalent to the administrative posts now available. There should be three pay increments above the maximum level in the teacher's present salary schedule for the master teacher, the highest equivalent to the headmaster's or principal's salary.
- Job descriptions should be developed that outline the general and unique qualifications essential for every administrative position in the Boston School Department (e.g., Area Superintendent for Dorchester, Principal for Higginson District).
- The biennial service mark should be eliminated from the promotional rating system. However, supervisors' reports on a candidate for a specific administrative post should be submitted to the appropriate area personnel board as part of a candidate's credentials.
- Certificate examinations for administrative positions should be eliminated. Instead, the school department should engage a professional testing agency to

---

[a]Vincent C. Nuccio and Richard J. Doyle, et al., A STUDY OF PROMOTIONAL POLICIES AND PROCEDURES IN THE BOSTON PUBLIC SCHOOLS under the Direction of the Committee of Deans of Schools of Education of Greater Boston, Center for Field Research and School Services, Boston College, April 1970.

compile examinations which would evaluate specific talents for specific positions.

- The Associate Superintendent's Personal Qualities Interview should be eliminated; instead, a panel of four outside consultants should interview and screen candidates for the assistant superintendency and for all city-wide posts.
- Each of the six districts should have a seven member personnel board composed of the district superintendent, two building level administrators, two teachers, and two parents. This board would review applications, interview candidates, and recommend individuals for specific positions. These six boards would also develop job descriptions for their district.
- The headmaster (or principal) should have major responsibility for selecting teachers, assistant principals, and department heads.
- The assistant superintendent should have primary authority to select headmasters and principals in his district. Personnel boards should make recommendations either to the assistant superintendent or to the headmaster/principal—whoever is appropriate for each vacancy.
- In cooperation with area universities, the Boston School Department should establish twenty-four administrative internships. Three interns should be assigned to each of the six districts, and six interns to the central administration. Interns could come from both inside and outside the system. This program could serve the dual purpose of recruiting and testing administrative talent.
- In-service training for all administrators is essential, especially for older, more experienced administrators who may be somewhat out of touch with new developments. Administrators at every level should be encouraged to take leaves of absence.
- Notice of specific vacancies, along with position descriptions, should be circulated inside and outside Boston schools. Applications for these jobs should be directed to the appropriate personnel board.
- The Boston School Department must search for able administrators—both locally and nationally. During the next decade, there will be about 300 vacancies; 50 at least of these vacancies should be filled by personnel from outside the Boston School Department. The department must abandon the present practice of making administrative appointments only from within the system.
- Principals, headmasters, and assistant superintendents should be hired on the basis of a six year, renewable contract. The deputy and associate superintendents should serve at the discretion of the superintendent.

The Boston School Study research supports the recommendations from the deans' study. The research also supports the idea of an Administrative Development Program in which all future principals and headmasters would participate (except for those with previous administrative experience outside the Boston School System).

This program should be operated by an Educational Administration Committee with the following members:

- The associate superintendent for personnel (chairman, no vote)
- The associate superintendent for staff and organizational development
- Two area superintendents (biennial election by area superintendents)
- One headmaster (biennial election by headmaster)
- One principal (biennial election by principals)
- One teacher (appointed by the union)
- Two paid outside consultants who are recognized leaders in educational administration (one appointed by superintendent, one elected by the committee)

No member except the chairman should serve for more than two consecutive years.

The committee should plan educational administration programs, admit candidates to the programs, and evaluate students during their studies and internships. Evaluation may include a student's dismissal from the program or a candidate's exemption from a segment of the program because of previous training.[b] The committee, aware of an individual's interests and proven abilities, will advise the superintendent that program graduates be nominated for consideration by personnel boards (and area superintendent) of specific schools.

Admission to the Program

To apply for admission, candidates must meet state certification requirements for principal or headmaster at a particular level (teacher certification at a chosen level, plus one eighteen-hour administration program). The candidate also must have served either three years in the Boston system, or three years in other school systems or educational enterprises such as an alternative school or counseling project.

Candidates should present information to the committee for evaluation. Rather than establishing in advance a set weight to any credential, the committee should evaluate items on individual bases. Advanced degrees do not indicate a candidate will be a good principal; similarly, top biennial service marks do not necessarily mean a fine teacher will be an effective administrator.

Three members of the Educational Administrative Committee should inter-

---

[b]If a trainee, for example, has recently completed formal graduate study, the committee may feel, after an evaluation of the candidate, that some Administrative Development courses would be repetitive.

view each candidate. These interviews should assess the credentials a candidate presents and evaluate his personality, enthusiasm, and suitability for educational leadership. The entire committee will vote admission to the program based on subcommittee recommendations; the entire committee may occasionally also vote certain program exemptions or revisions for individual candidates. One factor governing candidates admitted will be the number of anticipated vacancies in the next two years.

The Program

The following Administrative Development Program is designed to assure that candidates receive high-quality training and experience and that candidates are selected for positions in particular schools by continuuous observation and evaluation in academic and on-the-job activities.

First Year: Academic Phase. While employed at their regular post in the Boston School Department, trainees will attend afternoon or evening classes five to seven hours weekly. The program should be organized by the personnel officials with the assistance of the Administrative Development Committee and in cooperation with present headmasters/principals, local universities, and the trainees themselves. The school department should contract with education schools or professors at various institutions to offer, either themselves or in cooperation with school personnel, seminars in such areas as human relations/ sensitivity training, program development/evaluation, staff supervision, community-school relations, budget, union relations, etc.[c]

Written evaluation by each professor or group leader on a trainee's academic performance, personality, interest, and enthusiasm should become part of his file; midway and at the end of the year, the Administrative Development Committee should evaluate a candidate on the basis of this new information, discuss strengths and weaknesses with individuals, and eliminate less promising people from the program.

Second Year: Administrative Internships. Trainees should spend a ten-month period working in these areas:

- Two months as assistant to the principal in a school outside Boston
- One month in the central of a district office, or in a community service agency (August/September)
- One month as assistant principal in an elementary school (if he wants to become a high school principal), or as assistant principal in a high school or or junior high (if candidate wants to become an elementary principal)

---

[c]Some arrangement should be negotiated with universities so that degree credit might be granted on an individual basis.

- Six months in a school at the candidate's future level (two months as assistant principal; four months as acting principal)[d]

The AD Committee should receive and evaluate written summaries of the candidate's internships and discuss them with the candidate. Opinions of the candidate's acting principalship should be gathered from teachers, the district superintendent, parents, students, and community leaders. Evaluation at this stage of the program should serve to enlighten a candidate about his strengths and weaknesses and to assist the AD Committee in recommending the type of school to which a trainee ultimately should be assigned as principal.

Appointment to Job

No "rating list" should be established when the trainees have finished the program. The important decision is not who is best and who is worst among the candidates, but rather who is most qualified for the headmaster's or principal's post at a specific school at that time.

On the basis of dossier information, the AD Committee should suggest to the superintendent that he nominate from two to four candidates who have demonstrated interest and ability for a vacancy at a particular school. The Building Personnel Board would interview all the nominated candidates and the district superintendent would make the final decision.

Candidates awaiting permanent positions could be assigned as acting principals. This practice would provide opportunities for present principals to enroll in professional training programs.

To assure continued professional growth after appointment, no headmaster or principal should remain in his job for more than seven years without a paid, professional sabbatical. A sabbatical might be a teaching year in the AD Program's academic phase plus courses at a local university; full-time enrollment at a university; or a special assignment for another school system or the state. His study plans should be approved by the Board of Examiners and the district superintendent.

Associate superintendents, district superintendents, and directors of departments should not remain in their jobs more than seven years without a nine-month sabbatical to: hold a similar position in another school system; enroll as a full-time student in courses relevant to their professional fields; or hold a *different* position in the Boston system (e.g., an associate superintendent could teach for a year, an assistant superintendent could become acting principal in another district).

---

[d]While the fully certified trainee is acting principal, the present principal, at full salary, should either become a full-time student at a local university or a part-time student at a local university and participate in the academic part of the Administrative Development program.

Continuing Education for Educators

To respond to new situations and new problems, teachers, administrators, and specialists in the school department must have continuing in-service education. The Boston School Department offers periodic courses and workshops for its own personnel. Examples from recent years include:

- A course on race relations and the schools taught by a series of guest lecturers
- A workshop for principals on the legal rights of students, parents, and school personnel, with recent court decisions explained by a law department attorney
- Boston State College and Harvard-Boston summer courses emphasizing modern instructional approaches like team teaching

Furthermore, each principal meets once a month during the school year with other principals at his level (e.g., junior high) and once a month with other principals in his geographical area (e.g., Dorchester) to work on common problems, interpret new procedures, and acquire new information.

Recently the Mental Health Council has provided a forum for discussions and training of leaders of various special services—health, guidance, attendance, tests and measurements, etc. Resource persons from the Laboratory of Community Psychiatry and other agencies have provided useful information and ideas to staff members.

However, Boston school personnel—especially administrators—often lack up-to-date and useful knowledge in key areas:

- Program evaluation, using test data, using evaluation for planning, relating data to program revision and staff retraining. As a result, evaluation efforts are feared, sabotaged, criticized, or concealed, instead of being used to improve productivity.
- Data-processing, which most school officials do not know how to request or use. In some cases, directors of departments do not want to share information with other school departments that need it!
- Special services and special education, which many principals without much background in special education, regard the placement of a special class in their school as a punishment or penalty (e.g., for losing pupils and having extra space).
- Program and proposal development, especially to request help for children, who need new learning situations—for example, non-English speaking children. Many principals fail to use their authority to request additional paid staff or volunteers, extra equipment or money. Principals are not trained or encouraged to contribute ideas for federal or state programs, nor to try changing the share a school receives in the local school budget.

- Community relations, especially the handling of racial tensions and conflict. Some principals have shown great interest in working with community organizations, but other administrators will work only with the local Home and School Association.
- New ways of using space and materials. Too few principals or teachers are emotionally or educationally ready to use flexibility of new facilities in their work with children.

Boston school officials at all levels expressed concern about the capacity of universities to offer help in these and other areas. Local universities (with the possible exception of state colleges) tend to supply idealistic, but relatively untrained teachers for urban classrooms. Programs to prepare urban teachers are certainly deficient. Moreover, many university professors who train future teachers are unaware of the conditions in inner-city schools.

Progressive urban educators now advocate using a variety of urban schools to train future teachers and counselors. If professors do not join with school personnel, teacher training programs will continue to produce idealists with romantic notions about liberating urban children. In the past, Boston school officials have been disappointed by the failure of several major universities to provide the numbers of interns that schools request, to follow through on innovative programs, and to repeat successful programs for the training or retraining of inner-city school personnel. However, school officials still welcome thorough participation from universities.

At the same time, Boston school officials were reluctant to require directors or associate superintendents to complete advanced training or doctoral study in a relevant educational field (e.g., special education, psychology, planning, or evaluation of instruction). A few exceptions are found—some supervisor directors have earned doctorates. The previous superintendent encouraged at least half a dozen men to use additional leave for doctoral work at New York University, Stanford, Harvard, Boston University, and elsewhere. But the system did not support advanced training and mid-career leaves for study. Those who take time off for study are regarded as dropouts fleeing from the real world and losing their place in line for promotion. In other cities, comparable to Boston, advanced study through the doctorate is considered a necessity for administrators.

No one would argue that a doctorate alone provides sufficient competence to solve complex urban education problems. Some Boston school officials display courage and creativity which no doctoral degree can develop. But Boston schools deserve the best in training as well as the best in talent.

Boston area colleges and universities have different strengths and specialties which should be exploited—for example, Boston College—evaluation and research on instruction, Boston University—special education and guidance, Harvard—reading, planning and administration. Once Boston State College sponsored a valuable summer program which provided special training for prospective teachers of the disadvantaged. The two branches of the University of Massachusetts—Amherst and Boston—offer teacher retraining and curriculum development. M.I.T.'s potential, including the Sloan School of Management which has increased its scope to include education, has hardly been tapped, although in 1969-70, school system and university officials began preliminary discussions.

The Boston School Department provides a variety of services, including public health, mental health, recreation, transportation, and food services. Area universities and their schools of medicine, public health, law, business, and social welfare have begun to contribute ideas and faculty members and sponsor in-service training conferences and workshops in these noneducational areas. Some of the smaller liberal arts colleges, e.g., Emmanuel and Simmons, respond rapidly and constructively to needs in specialized areas, such as the teaching of English as a second language and school library services.

Some private firms specialize in in-service training. During this study a few private firms were involved in staff training in Boston:

- The Management Analysis Center of Washington, D.C. conducted a workshop attended by Boston school directors on a program planning, budgeting, evaluation system (PPBES).
- The Management Formation Company of New York City led a series of discussions on minority recruitment for Boston school staff members.
- McBer and Company (formerly the Behavioral Science Center) of Cambridge arranged a workshop on the concepts and tools of organizational development and renewal.

The Educational Development Center (Newton) and the Education Collaborative (EDCO) also provide valuable staff training opportunities.

The burden of defining needs and of finding the right opportunities for staff development must be on the Boston School Department:

- One Associate Superintendent must assume major responsibility for staff and organizational development.
- Priorities will change each year but five areas of concern (evaluation, data processing, special services, proposal development, and community relations) should be emphasized. Area Superintendents, principals, directors and teachers should generate additional ideas. In-service training should be linked to curriculum development.
- Administrators and staff members of new schools should have at least a month to learn how to maximize the educational success of facilities and spaces.
- School administrators and specialists should be encouraged and rewarded

financially for one and two year mid-career professional leaves for full-time advanced study, especially in technical areas like planning, evaluation, special services, and vocational education.

- Boston should collaborate with other school systems to use colleges and universities, private firms, metropolitan and regional education agencies in staff training.

The Office of Staff and Organizational Development should seek funds from a variety of sources: federal, state and local business firms, and Boston area foundations. Colleges, universities, and other agencies should apply for public funds if the city school system urges them to co-sponsor a needed program or workshop. The same office should publicize and counsel school system employees about fellowships and other possibilities for advanced study.

Minority Recruitment

In the past few years, strengthened by the increased flexibility the National Teachers Exam gives recruiters, the director of personnel, the administrative assistant to the superintendent, the Board of Examiners, and their associates in the school department have expanded their efforts to attract oustanding educators to the Boston schools. Boston recruitment brochures and related materials have been sent to over 600 accredited colleges, and each year school representatives have visited over 48 institutions in the New England area in this expanded search for candidates. These efforts, combined with a recent nationwide surplus of teachers and the attractiveness of the Boston area, have produced dramatic results: the number of applicants has grown from 1,298 (1963), to 1,670 (1965), to 2,005 (1967), to 2,900 (1969)—more than a 200 percent increase over a seven-year period.

This recruitment program has enabled Boston to become more selective in choosing personnel entering the system. But these efforts have failed to attract minority group candidates to Boston. In an attempt to improve minority recruitment, the school department in 1969 sent brochures and other materials to forty-nine predominantly black colleges, and advertised in the teacher recruitment supplement of AFRO-AMERICAN NEWSPAPERS, a publication distributed on ninety-five black campuses. Also, two blacks and two whites from Boston personally visited Bowery State, Coppins State, D.C. Teacher's College, Hampton Institute, Norfolk State, Virginia State and Old Dominion College to encourage students to apply for jobs in the Boston schools.

Unfortunately, only two blacks joined the school department as a result of these efforts. The original newspaper publishing schedule was delayed, making it difficult for candidates to meet the application deadline. And at black colleges the recruiters visited, they discovered that many scholarship students were committed to teach in their home states for one or two years after graduation. The school department .*must* dramatically alter and expand its efforts in minority-group recruitment.

Of the $5,000 teachers and administrators in the system, fewer than 250 in 1970 (less than 5 percent) were black; Boston's black student population was 27,280—30 percent of the total enrollment. Almost 40 percent of the first-graders in Boston are black. Only a handful of teachers and administrators are native Spanish-speaking. Black representation among the upper echelons of the school department is almost nonexistent. Until 1972 none of the six associate superintendents was black. Until just before this report came out in 1970, none of the six district superintendents was black. And no one at the superintendency-level in Boston had a black assistant. Blacks hold only four of the more than ninety principalships in the city. There are some black assistant directors, but all thirty-four directors of departments are white.

Some changes are underway. Although only three blacks applied for the most recent two principal ratings, two of these men were named to the Principalship. Of the ninety-seven finalists in the June, 1969 rating for assistant principal, seven were black—five blacks finished in the top twenty, and six of the seven black finalists have already been named assistant principals. And because more black students have recently enrolled in Boston and Massachusetts colleges, more state residents should be applying to work in Boston schools within the next two years.

The following steps should be taken to assure more black representation at *all* levels in the Boston School Department. This goal is necessary to provide role models for black children; to enable blacks to view schools as part of their community; to foster greater sensitivity in the schools to the needs and aspirations of all the citizens of Boston; to give nonblack children the advantage of having outstanding black and white teachers; and finally, to achieve an excellence and sophistication in the educational system which a great city deserves and which only true diversity of students *and staff* can accomplish.

Recommendations

Boston recruiters should visit more and different colleges in the search for black talent. They should concentrate on schools in large cities which have a high percentage of black population and a recognition of urban problems. A few promising sources are Michigan State University, the University of Wisconsin, the Atlanta College complex in Georgia, the University of Chicago, Roosevelt University (Chicago), the University of Illinois, New York University and the City University of New York (CUNY).

The school department should not limit its search to the resources of the placement office at host colleges. Many blacks either never register at their college placement office or use this service sparingly. By contacting and visiting fraternities and sororities on all-black campuses as well as black student associations on mixed campuses, Boston recruiters might discover a rich source of talent few other employers have tapped. The interest and initiative these efforts indicate would give Boston considerable advantage in hiring sought-after students.

Recruitment personnel, both black and white, must be the most articulate, enthusiastic, persuasive, and vigorous representatives of the Boston school system. Special efforts should be made to recruit black candidates trained in math, science, home economics and special education, not English and social studies where the list is already full.

The recruitment team should be authorized to invite outstanding black candidates to visit Boston at the school department's expense. Members of the local black community could act as co-hosts to explain the problems and strengths of the city and its schools to candidates. Black citizen participation in recruitment could provide valuable feedback about candidates from community members to the school department.

The Boston School Department should place recruitment advertisements in black publications that educational recruiters do not ordinarily use. This step would demonstrate Boston's interest and would reach practicing black professionals in other urban school systems. These newspapers include: The AMSTERDAM NEWS, the CHICAGO DEFENDER, the ATLANTA WORLD, and the BAY STATE BANNER. Among other things, these advertisements should stress the opportunity for Boston teachers to continue their educations at a variety of area schools.

Regardless of how ambitious or successful Boston's black recruitment effort is in the next few years, the school department should (and did) take *immediate* steps to seek out and promote blacks to visible, responsible leadership positions in the system. Black teachers also need professional role models to convince them of the system's legitimacy and sincerity.

Boston should appoint a black administrative aide as assistant to the superintendent. At least one new associate and area superintendent should be black (accomplished as of 1972). Area superintendents should try to assemble integrated staffs. As principalships and heads of department positions become available, the school department must work to assure that qualified blacks apply. The Department should first seek out and encourage minority persons presently in the system to apply for these positions. The school department should help an especially able black candidate fill any "technical" qualification he may lack, by providing training at a local university. To draw immediately on outstanding outside talent, the Boston School Department should consult with Richard Clark, Associates (NYC) or Management Formation, Inc. (NYC), agencies which specialize in identifying outstanding black professionals.

To assist in the recruitment program, the school department should consider:

encouraging outstanding high school seniors to consider a future teaching career in Boston by establishing a teaching apprenticeship program, with credit; offering equal credit to incoming teachers for service in A.C.T.I.O.N., the Teacher Corps or in other school systems; increasing the number of paraprofessionals in the schools, drawn from the community and from local colleges (see the section on mixed staffing); offering preexamination tutoring on a voluntary basis; and emphasizing to local colleges that Boston wishes to hire more black student teachers.

Obviously, many recommendations in other sections of this report apply to black recruitment, directly or indirectly. However, one recommendation deserves special emphasis: When Boston school leaders are recruiting at a college, attending an educational conference, or visiting another school system, they need the authority and flexibility to immediately encourage a particularly able educator about a job in Boston. Therefore, the superintendent should have the discretion to hire a certain number of highly qualified professionals without requiring that they pass through a series of promotional steps.

The question of hiring Spanish personnel is also vital, because at least 3 percent (3,200) of the city's student population is Spanish-speaking; it is widely believed that the potential student population in the Spanish community is several times larger. Many of the specific proposals as well as the spirit of the recruitment strategy for blacks also applies to hiring and promoting Spanish-speaking educators. The hiring of a Spanish-speaking administrator in 1972 as a top assistant was an important first step, but no substitute for bilingual administrators for at least a dozen schools and other key assignments.

Boston must "mount an individualized, energetic, systematic, and visible effort to convince the qualified minority group member that ... [they] want and can use his specific skills, talent, or potential. A fringe benefit of such a credibility breakthrough is that the word quickly circulates in the minority group community that one of their own has been hired to a position of responsibility, thus motivating others to seek employment ... on their own initiative.[e]

Labor Relations in Boston

The Boston School Committee negotiates with seven employee groups. The teachers form the largest groups, although they are only recently organized. Custodians, secretaries, lunchroom workers, and other nonacademic employees also bargain for wages and employment conditions.

The 1970 teachers strike highlights the importance not only of able negotiators on both sides but of an impasse procedure to resolve key points during, not after, the period of budget preparation.

---

[e]Ulric Haynes, Jr., "Equal Job Opportunity: the Credibility Gap," THE HARVARD BUSINESS REVIEW, May-June, 1968, p. 114.

Negotiation is more than a school committee responsibility. Staff relations under a negotiated contract require year-round discussions, studies, problem-solving, and grievance resolution. Personnel officers must train all administrators and they must annually brief each principal and director on procedures under new contracts.

Recommendations

- Massachusetts should adopt a feature of the New York State Taylor Law, which ties contract negotiations of public employees to the budget cycle and calls for outside mediation if the teachers' contract is not signed sixty days before the budget, according to law, must be finally set.
- The school committee should consider the superintendent and associate superintendent for personnel responsible for the preparations for negotiations, involvement of staff in study committees, conduct of negotiating, and follow-up training of staff, using staff assistance from the coordinator of staff relations and labor relations consultant.
- Teachers and other school employees should be consulted on all policy and procedural changes, such as those suggested in this report, because teachers have a stake in making the system more effective. Also, contracts with teachers and other employees will need continuous review and revision to implement many of the recommendations.

The Overall Organization

Boston currently has a Board of Superintendents chaired by the superintendent and including the business manager and six associate superintendents, one of whom is designated as the deputy superintendent. Three of the associate superintendents have specialized responsibilities: one for all academic personnel; one for curriculum, university relations, planning of new facilities, and program development; and one for special education and some related pupil services. Three of the associates in 1970 exercised authority over a level of the system—elementary, junior high, and senior high. At the same time, each principal and school is supervised by an area superintendent assigned on a geographic basis.

Thus each principal has two formal superiors, both of whom conduct monthly meetings. Directives initialed by one must be interpreted by the other. In times of emergencies, both the appropriate associate and area superintendent must be notified.

The concept of the area superintendent places a responsible decision-maker in a field office near the school site and in close touch with the neighborhoods. But unlike their counterparts in other cities, area superintendents have no supporting staff. They can attend only a fraction of the community and agency meetings at which the school department should be represented, and it is very difficult for them to work closely with principals and specialists to respond to local educational needs. At the same time, most of the area superintendents have been assigned system-wide responsibilities to ease the load on certain associate superintendents.

For the past two years, the most severe organizational bottleneck in the Boston School Department has been the special services area—the revision of the many pupil services and special educational programs. These services require full-time attention from a qualified specialist.

Another serious problem is the expansion of system-wide planning of curricula and new school facilities. These two planning functions must be coordinated but each may require a separate high level administrator, especially as the system increases its commitment to planning.

Too many top administrators share responsibilities for day-to-day operations. Too few administrators are free for long-range planning or development of new and more responsive educational programs. The men and women in these roles emphasize that they spend most of their time trouble-shooting and reacting to crises. Associate superintendents should assume new planning and service roles; the area superintendent's decision-making authority should be increased.

Associate superintendents would provide leadership in the following service areas:

- Personnel—recruitment, placement and evaluation
- Curriculum and instruction
- Educational planning—demographic, physical, financial
- Special services and system evaluation
- Staff and organizational development
- Field operations—coordination among areas.

The Personnel Function

The personnel function of the Boston Public Schools was badly fragmented:

- An administrative assistant to the superintendent heads teacher recruiting.
- The secretary of the school committee (not the Personnel Department) nominally assigns and supervises all secretaries, clerks, and lunch aides in the system.
- The custodians, selected by civil service, report directly to the school committee—a relationship that encourages old-style patronage politics.
- Other civil service personnel—lunchroom workers, attendance officers, etc.— are dispersed in various departments other than Personnel.
- The coordinator of negotiations and staff relations reports directly to the school committee.
- The associate superintendent for personnel is concerned with the assignment, transfer, promotion, and retirement of professional staff.

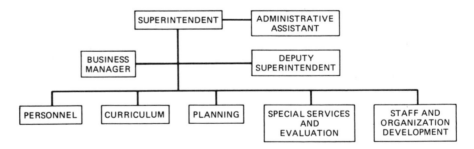

Figure 6-1. Staff Organization for the Boston Schools 1970 Proposal.

A review of other large city school systems indicates that the recruitment, selection, assignment, and movement of all personnel other than the superintendent should be coordinated by a single personnel office. At the same time, principals, directors, and department heads should have more responsibility in recruitment and selection, and parents should have greater influence in selecting a principal.

The associate superintendent for personnel should coordinate all efforts to recruit and select academic and nonacademic staff, professional and civil service staff. He should work with directors, area superintendents, principals, parent groups, and others to devise appropriate criteria to evaluate the performance of all staff members (annually for three years and then at least every three years). He should be in charge of planning and revising personnel procedures, salary and wage scales, and employee negotiations.

Gradually, the Board of Examiners has become a personnel recruitment team, working with directors and specialists to attract teachers to Boston. Their formal work with examinations would decrease as teachers take the National Teachers Examination and as directors and specialists are selected with help from expert panels as the deans recommended in 1970.[1] The examiners should be reclassified as educational personnel specialists. They should assist the associate superintendent in recruiting, selecting, assigning, transferring, and counseling individual teachers on personnel matters (leave policy, advancement in the system, salary adjustments, retirement, etc.). By 1975 the board should not exist as an administrative or legal entity. The associate superintendent will need two personnel assistants for elementary and secondary professional staff and a supervisor of nonacademic personnel. He will also need civil service personnel, with at least two clerks to handle applications, paper work, and job specification and recruitment efforts.

The coordinator for negotiations and staff relations should work with the school committee and its labor relations consultant, but the associate superintendent should be in charge of planning for contract review, for implementing contracts, developing handbooks for new personnel, and supervising the orientation of principals and directors.

Custodians should no longer work directly for the Committee and, like other employees, be prohibited, by regulation or statute, from political campaigning for the school committee candidates.

The Curriculum and Instruction Function

Presently, the curriculum development department is separate from many of the subject matter departments. Partly to equalize responsibilities, four of the associate superintendents are in charge of specific subjects and skill areas. Review and revitalization of the curriculum should be the job of teachers and principals, universities personnel, and concerned citizens, students, and counselors.

The various departments which deal with instruction (other than special education) should be grouped together. Program development and improving teacher skills should be linked—teachers should learn new concepts and teaching techniques *while* they are developing new instructional programs in their schools, cities, states, or regions.

An associate superintendent for curriculum and instruction should provide general leadership in evaluating and planning instruction for Boston children, according to their varied needs and talents. This associate would recommend various alternative programs and direct staff to help teachers evaluate learning materials. An administrative assistant would help teachers and other staff get information they need. Teaching staffs and parents should know the results of program evaluation and plans for revision.

Educational Planning

Until the late 1960s the Boston School Department had little incentive for systematic educational planning. The school population was declining and dozens of older facilities were closed or consolidated. Also, other city agencies and a separate school house commission were responsible for facilities planning.

Recently, however, Boston has planned more than thirty new schools. The school department has two agencies with responsibility for planning, an Educational Planning Center and an Office of Planning and Engineering (formerly the Chief Structural Engineer and staff).

The planning function has grown more complex. Boston schools must be planned with the State Department of Education, the redevelopment planners and the public facility planners. State, federal, and foundation funds are available in many instances. Furthermore, parent and citizen groups insist on participating in planning facilities in their communities.

The largest and most obvious need is for new physical facilities. But planning also requires program evaluation and projections to develop specialized facilities like the Occupational Resources Center. Planning requires an analysis of relevant demographic trends like the effect of conditions in the Puerto Rican economy on migration to Boston. Planning requires identifying needs for new staff or staff skills to use technology or new space configurations. Planning requires assessing parent and neighborhood attitudes and searching for new approaches to education, including the use of nonschool resources (cultural centers, businesses, museums, hospitals). Parents and children have a right to expect a broader definition of education in the future.

The associate superintendent for planning should be responsible for demographic and statistical studies necessary to anticipate demands for educational programs and facilities. He should be the school department's major liaison with other city and state planning officers and agencies, and he should prepare proposals for financing from city, state, federal, and private sources.

As the chief planning officer, this associate should be responsible for two of the most challenging tasks to confront the school department: preparing, with other states and local school systems, plans to comply with the Racial Imbalance Act; and making provisions for the effects of parochial school closings in Boston.

Special Services

During 1969 and 1970 Boston school officials spent considerable time reviewing the need to revise procedures and policies in the special services. Court suits forced the school system to question placement and testing policies. Meanwhile, a MACE task force offered new guidelines for the state and school systems and paved the way for a major change in the special education statutes.

Once, the post of associate superintendent for special services in Boston had been regarded as an impossible assignment and even a form of punishment. Many decisions must be made closer to the level of the school site, the child, and the neighborhood mental health clinic's multiservice agency. The associate must lead by decentralizing many pupil services to the area level.

The following job requirements and description have been prepared in consultation with state and local experts.

The associate superintendent for special services should have these responsibilities:

- Developing, directing, coordinating, and evaluating all activities in the special services area
- Supervising and evaluating the special services staff
- Developing relevant in-service training for staff
- Making recommendations to the superintendent concerning desirable policies, revision of policies and the further development of special services
- Maintaining a close working relationship with other district-wide administrators and other programs
- Using the resources of other agencies in the community and expanding the skills of the present staff
- Providing an organized decision-making process

The associate should nominate to the superintendent two assistants and all department directors within this organizational jurisdiction and be able to choose at least 15 percent of his staff from nonrated personnel to bring in experienced people from other youth-serving agencies.

Staff and Organizational Development

There is far too little systematic evaluation at all levels of the school system. Organizational changes are made either periodically (once every five to twenty years) or as a result of a crisis. Not enough emphasis is placed on systematic and continuous change according to need. Associate superintendents have largely abdicated their managerial roles. As a result, those below them (especially department directors) are not encouraged to plan, or to initiate and evaluate change.

Interviews and the consensus of the Organization Development Workshop[a] indicate that many Boston educators want the system to anticipate the need for change not merely react to change.

An Associate Superintendent for Staff and Organizational Development should have these responsibilities:

- Training programs for all school personnel on matters having to do with staff development, in-service training, orientation programs and organizational improvement. This might include workshops on improving organizational communication, problem-solving capabilities, conflict management, and goal-setting.
- Consulting with any organizational unit in the system which has organizational problems and requests help.
- Recommending structural changes for the entire system.
- Suggesting new processes for organizational improvement in the system (e.g., more collaboration between units, team building, a new way to manage conflict between certain units).
- Helping with personnel problems associated with planning, evaluation, and change. Helping to reduce resistance and facilitate implementation.
- Helping to identify factors in the external environment (the city, business, other agencies) and in the school system which have implications for organizational changes.

He should work closely with all of the associate and area superintendents, but especially with the associate superintendents for personnel and planning who would have complementary but different responsibilities.

With the superintendent, the associate superintendents would form a special committee to propose and plan for the major self-renewal activities of the system. These plans would later be proposed to the school committee for its approval. The associate superintendent should have at least two assistants skilled at planning conferences, workshops, and in-service courses, and at working with directors and principals. Current staff of the Department of Supervision should work as part of this staff on an area basis as resource teachers.

[a]About twenty-five administrators at all levels and five teachers from the school system participated in an OD workshop at Harvard University June 3-4, 1970.

The associate superintendent should have these qualifications:

- Experience in organizational analysis and change and in conducting in-service programs for school personnel
- At least three graduate courses in organizational change from an accredited university (courses given at the Sloan School of Management, M.I.T., and the Human Relations Center, B.U., are recommended)
- Skill in interpersonal relations, open and honest communication, collaboration, conflict-resolution, and the ability to listen to and use constructive feedback

This associate would work closely with EDCO (Education Collaborative), universities, and firms which specialize in staff retraining and organizational renewal. He would work with personnel officials, area superintendents, directors, principals, and others to prepare people for new programs, new buildings, and new responsibilities.

Field Operations

Currently, the responsibility for day-to-day operation of the school system is divided among the three associates for various levels and the area superintendents whose council is chaired by a fourth associate.

A deputy for field operations should coordinate the work of the area superintendents who would make virtually all decisions about the schools in their areas. This deputy would provide support for the superintendent in times of emergencies, would expedite necessary repairs and other actions needed to maintain the schools, and would supervise the area superintendents work with community and parent groups. He would provide opportunities for principals to meet frequently with other staff members.

The Business Manager

In Boston, the business manager is responsible for the budget, accounts, payroll, inventories and supplies, and recommendations to the school committee about possible economies and efficiencies.

The Boston school business manager serves on the Board of Superintendents and is paid at the same salary level as the deputy superintendent, thus establishing him as one of the three most important men in the school system.

Boston differs from many other large cities because it separates other business-related services like the school lunch program, school transportation, school custodians, and plant maintenance and operations from the business manager's jurisdiction.

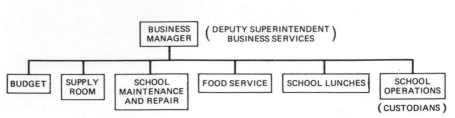

Figure 6-2. Business Functions of the Boston Schools.

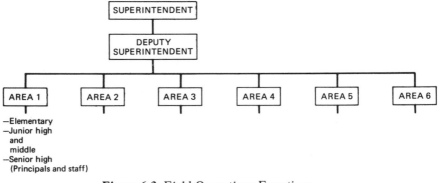

Figure 6-3. Field Operations Functions.

The school lunch program director in 1970 reported to the associate superintendent for junior high schools. School transportation personnel reported to another superintendent. School custodians report directly to the school committee, a Boston relationship unique to American education and to governing boards generally (and suggesting a special privilege and political relationship that undermines public confidence in the school committee). Plant maintenance personnel, supervised by the chief structural engineer, report directly to the superintendent—again, a unique historical tradition unsupported by logic or by notions of efficient or effective service. The alterations and repair budget, which *does not* reveal specific projects and priorities, has been a major political football for previous school committees, undermining teaching and learning conditions in Boston schools.

In San Francisco, the associate superintendent for business assumes responsibilities not only for fiscal affairs and budget planning, but for building maintenance and repair (major and minor), food service, and data processing.

In San Diego, an assistant superintendent for business supervises maintenance, operations (including custodians), food services, construction, and purchasing and general business services. A related administrative services division prepares the budgets, coordinates plans, public information, and related services. Both divisions are under an associate superintendent with Deputy rank who coordinates school services.

In Los Angeles one deputy superintendent coordinates instruction and education, and another deputy organizes the business, budget, school planning and administrative services.

The Philadelphia deputy superintendent for administrator's services coordinates the work of directors of business services, data processing, facilities, finance and, personnel. The director of business services is in charge of food services, the purchasing division, transportation, and the warehouse. The facilities division, headed by an associate superintendent, coordinates planning, construction, land acquisition, and maintenance and operations.

In most cities, business services generally include food services, school maintenance, and custodial operations. Those city school departments that build their own schools sometimes include repairs with plant planning. But in Boston a separate agency builds the schools and no one wants another agency to handle schoolhouse repairs.

School business functions should be consolidated under a business manager whose competence, integrity, and efficiency is unquestioned. The directors of school lunch and transportation (formerly safety), the custodians, and the chief structural engineer shall be designated assistant business managers at no loss in pay.

At the same time the business manager should have additional staff in order to use a program budget. His office would require at least five budgetary and evaluative analysts.

In summary, the Business Manager (or Deputy Superintendent for Business Services) would continue to be the chief budgetary coordinator. He would be responsible for accounts, fiscal controls, supplies and inventories. He would assume general supervision of food services, transportation, school custodial operations and maintenance and repairs.

The Chief Schoolhouse Custodian would become Director of Plant Maintenance with the rank of assistant business manager. This would not prevent him from making prompt responses to emergencies, taking appropriate disciplinary steps, or establishing training opportunities for custodians. No longer would custodians need to influence school committee members by attending school committee meetings as a group and by operating as a power block in school committee elections.

The alterations and repair budget would become a much more detailed document with area-by-area projects listed by schools (painting, renovations, planned repairs of roofs, gutters, masonry) and a reserve for emergencies. Responsibility for site acquisition, for new schools and other planning would be under the jurisdiction of the associate superintendent for planning.

Planning for an expanded food services program and for additional pupil transportation would occur in the planning office in close coordination with school business officials.

Implications for Departments

Changes in the responsibilities of associate superintendents should enable the system to become more efficient. The planning function would be transformed from the part-time concern of one associate superintendent to the full-time occupation of one and a consideration of many of the others. Program and personnel evaluation would become more significant.

Meanwhile, much of the work done by associate superintendents at the various levels (senior high, junior high, and elementary) would be assigned to area superintendents. Area superintendents would work with the associate for field operations but they would have substantial autonomy and freedom to encourage innovation and diversity in area schools and in districts.

Other assignments by levels (e.g., kindergarten, vocational education, and other departments) could be logically distributed among the associate superintendents. Some areas such as compensatory programs, physical education, and data processing require kindergarten-to-grade twelve coordination.

Departments would be grouped as follows:

Personnel

Examiners (became personnel specialists)
Teacher placement
Negotiators (staff relations)

Curriculum

Office of curriculum development
Audio-visual education and libraries
Kindergarten (becomes early childhood education)
Fine arts, music
Compensatory education
Science, reading, etc.

Planning

Educational planning center
Data Processing and statistics
Racial imbalance
Parochial school liason
Special projects and proposals

Special Services

Special Programs:
>Mentally retarded,
>Sensory disorders (incorporating vision resources, speech and hearing, perceptually handicapped),
>Emotionally disturbed,
>Physically handicapped

Pupil Services:
>Child guidance,
>Pupil adjustment counselors,
>Attendance (officers and child advocates),
>Health services (medical and mental health)

Staff and Organizational Development

Inservice courses, new staff orientation supervision
Teacher Supervision resource teachers
University liaison
Regional lab (EDC) and educational television
EDCO, NESDEC
New departments, programs and schools

Deputy for Field Operations

Area superintendents
Liaison with fire, police, Office of Human Rights
Representative of the superintendent
Legislative Relations

Deputy for Business Services

Budget and Accounts
Controls
Purchasing and supplies
School lunches
Transportation
Operations
Maintenance and repair

Implications for Area Superintendents and the Superintendency

This reorganization would make area superintendents responsible for the work of principals, headmasters, and faculties in their areas.

The superintendent currently has two administrative assistants, one who is responsible for communications and one who handles several problems including recruiting teachers and serving on the racial imbalance task force. In the revised organization, recruitment efforts would be handled by the associate for personnel and work on the imbalance task force by the associate for planning. One assistant should continue to help the superintendent with communications.

The second assistant could assume many of the responsibilities of legislative liaison which the deputy superintendent now has in cooperation with the superintendent and school committee. This work includes reviewing legislation which might affect the department, arranging for testimony, keeping track of individual bills, and informing school officials of relevant state and federal policy developments. Although testimony often requires the presence of the superintendent or deputy, one of the two assistants can, in approximately one third of his time, handle most of the detailed work.

The six associates, the business managers, and the superintendent form a Board of Superintendents which meets at least four times a month (sometimes twice each day) to take formal action on proposals for system-wide change. The board reviews and makes cuts in the budget, interviews and rates candidates for administrative promotion, and discusses solutions to specific and general problems. Until recently, the median age of this group has been the mid-sixties.

The Board is considered a graveyard for innovative ideas and proposals for change which might disturb vested interests.

A superintendents cabinet should replace this board. It would be an advisory group for resolving the many questions of planning, evaluation and coordination which will arise.

The cabinet should meet less often—weekly sessions for one-half day during the school year would be adequate. This would free the associates for more work with directors and principals. The median age of the board has recently dropped sharply because of the appointment of three mid-career innovative educators.

The cabinet proposal would further reduce the veto power of any set of administrators. Cabinet members would *not* interview all candidates for promotion to administrative positions. Furthermore, as many administrative and personnel decisions as possible would move to the levels of the school and area, freeing the central office staff for planning and evaluative activities.

The superintendent would continue to serve as chief executive and primary advisor to the school committee. Traditionally, Boston School Superintendents have remained fairly quiet at school committee meetings except when they are asked to present nominations for appointments. Instead, the superintendent should explain each agenda item and agressively offer the staff recommendations before school committee discussion. The school committee chairman in every instance should request the recommendation of the superintendent before a vote on agenda items.

Presently, the superintendent is not expected to comment on certain nonacademic matters, like the need for a custodial supervisory post or the selection of consultants. This practice denies the chief executive role. Jobs should not be created or contracts made without the recommendations of the chief executive—exceptions would be overall system evaluation and the selection of the superintendent himself.

Implementing a School System Reorganization Plan

Any reorganization of a large system requires time and energy. The system must complete certain parts of the plan before it can take other actions:

- Associate superintendents' assignments can be regrouped (as in fact was done) by fall 1970.
- Area superintendents need staff assistants before they can assume supervision, program development and budgeting responsibilities. The budgets should reflect the gradual strengthening of this role.
- Directors in some instances should assume greater responsibility; in other cases they may serve one or two years until their retirement or reassignment. Some might prefer to be special consultants or senior staff associates to assist with reorganization.
- Assistant directors and associate directors should not lose pay because of organizational changes.
- Several work conferences should be scheduled at the outset of any reorganization and at intervals thereafter, to discuss problems, develop solutions, and plan for contingencies and for a smooth transfer of functions. The Educational Planning Center should prepare detailed plans for the transition period and for implementation of reorganization plans. Key staff members might need four or five day sessions to plan the transition. One or more organizational consultants could assist the staff.
- Many of the proposed changes would require cooperation from teachers' unions and other school employee groups. Some groups would lose high wages, fancy titles, and privileged access to the school committee. But the largest number of teachers would gain time and resources if funds are redistributed for salaries, aides, and services students and teachers need. Almost all of the changes demand consultation with employees. Some changes require legislative support to pass; others require contract renegotiation over the next few years.
- The several tiers of school councils could be expanded over a two-year period. This expansion should not be delayed until statutory changes in the composition of the school committee take effect, which may be as late as 1974 unless the mayor, council, and General Court act with unusual dispatch (the mayor did not, therefore resulting in a delay).

- Parent and citizen groups would require information about changes in decision-making and expected benefits. Area superintendents, principals and headmasters would have special responsibilities to inform the public about reorganization plans.

The Problems of Planning

Previous studies, primarily those conducted by Cyril Sargent in 1953-54 and 1962-63, have documented the urgent need for new school facilities in Boston. More than fifty antiquated Boston school buildings have been closed and one dozen new facilities have been built since 1953, including two in 1969 and one during the 1970-71 school year. More than thirty new school buildings are currently being planned to replace sixty old, smaller, and less adaptable buildings.

In Boston, replacing nineteenth-century buildings (the oldest was built in 1847) must remain a high priority. However, demographic trends must be charted, interpreted, and taken into consideration when schools are planned. Age, sex, race, language, and ability levels of children are among the factors which determine the need for educational programs and facilities.

The Boston school system has begun to develop planning capabilities. As many as two dozen staff planners and consultants have been assigned to the Educational Planning Center. Their functions include community liaison work with neighborhoods which need new schools, short-range planning for school emergencies, and preparing proposals to qualify schools for federal funds.

But the planning effort, although it is gathering momentum, suffers from fragmented organization. The EPC is physically separate from the rest of the school administration. It overlaps to an extent with an Office of Planning and Engineering which finds school sites and prepares technical specifications and maps. A Statistics Office collects data and reports department responsibilities. The Data Processing Center is another separate office. The Statistics Office and the DPC report to the associate superintendent for high schools, the EPC reports to the associate for curriculum, and the chief engineer reports directly to the superintendent.

School planning efforts which do not involve local school and community leaders often meet with considerable criticism, both in the planning stage and immediately after the schools open. Some conflict over objectives, design and multiuse facilities (e.g., community rooms, pools) is inevitable. But planners must learn to identify and use community ideas. Currently both the EPC and the Public Facilities Department assign staff members to certain projects. However, community spokesmen criticize the absence of school representatives from many meetings.

Urban planners have developed many useful approaches to community participation in school planning:

- Staff of the Harvard-Boston Schools Planning Project, when preparing specifications for the new Kent School in Charlestown, not only conferred with educators and parents but asked children to draw pictures of the ideal school.
- M.I.T. and Harvard planners have developed techniques of advocate planning which provide poor and working class families with advocates who can fight for their rights and interests.
- Federal funds have been used to test out a concept called the charette, a lengthy session (week or weekend) in which educators, parents, students, city officials, neighborhood leaders and others collaborate in designing one or more facilities. A week long charette was held in Watertown, Massachusetts during winter 1970.

At the same time, school planning has moved in creative directions:

- Recognizing the need for small, specialized facilities to help develop model systems for general education, for language students, and for students who want and deserve more freedom, like the Murray Road Annex in Newton;
- Supporting multiple uses of space; placing a school in a larger office building or apartment, with options or rights to more space if needed; and
- Considering the twelve month and twenty-four hour school, to encourage adult and general community use on a week-long, year-round basis.

Several large city school systems are moving children into the city itself—into shops, business offices, museums, health centers, mass media offices and other institutions where adults work, learn, and can teach. In Philadelphia, 10,000 students applied to enter a parkway program which uses the varied resources of one section of the city.

Boston school staffs and planners developed Copley High School in Boston, as part of the Model Subsystem senior high component. Boston has a variety of hospitals, museums, insurance companies, and other organizations where courses in family health, aesthetics, and risk-taking could be taught. The Parkway Program enrolls 500 students and estimates that the city has saved $20 million by not building a new high school. The program requires only a relatively small staging area and a two man office. Instruction takes place in the various institutions which participate in the program. The Flexible Campus program in the early 1970s represents positive action on these ideas.

Recommendations for Boston

One associate superintendent for planning should coordinate the work of what is now the Educational Planning Center, the statistics Office (a new director would not be needed), and the planning function of the Engineering Office, which with the new state and additional city funds should concentrate on maintaining, repairing, and rehabilitating schools.

- The EPC needs educators (trained as teachers), statisticians, specification specialists, community advocate planners, and other technical specialists with training in planning and liaison work with communities and architects.
- A school planning council selected by parents in neighborhoods affected by new schools should advise planners from initial inception to final construction of a facility. Other parents, children, teachers, and interested parties should participate in planning workshops or charettes to settle differences of opinion.
- Planners should develop new programs through alliances with other institutions—for example, hospitals, prisons, television stations and the New England Aquarium—extending existing cooperation with the Children's Museum, Boston Symphony Orchestra, Woburn Gardens, Jordan Marsh and Filenes Department Stores each December, and other city institutions. For elementary and secondary students, Boston should develop "Downtown" and "Fenway Programs" which use the resources of the city. These flexible campus programs would require very little space, trust in students, cooperation from responsible adults, and the acceptance by colleges of a variety of learning experiences to qualify for admission.
- Boston should add city funds to strengthen the EPC, which in turn should continue to seek state, federal, and foundation grants. The EPC staff should work closely with other agencies that have planning staffs (e.g., BRA, Model Cities) to pioneer new approaches to education for Boston children and adults.

The task of planning new school buildings is complicated by the need to absorb students from parochial schools which are closing or may close in the next five years. More planning must be done to respond to the special needs of Spanish-speaking Cubans and Puerto Ricans, French-speaking Haitians, and an expanded Chinese population. Other major changes in the system—for example new instructional technology or the design of a totally new occupational education program—will require major leadership commitment from the associate superintendent for planning.

Parochial and Nonpublic Schools

A national survey of Catholic schools in the mid-1960s included the observation that, like the Rocky Mountains, an institution as massive as the parochial school system was not likely to disappear in the near future.

During 1970 a special report by the New England Catholic Education Center for the Archdiocese of Boston indicated that many parochial schools occupied substandard facilities and that by 1980 the Archdiocese might operate schools for only 50 percent of the 1970 enrollment.

During the 1960s several parochial schools in the city of Boston closed or consolidated. Since the 1930s as many as 40,000 children of school age—slightly less than one-third of all eligible Boston children—have annually attended nonpublic schools, most of them under Catholic sponsorship.

Other reports have catalogued the reasons for parochial school closings—the decline in religious vocations, increased costs of lay teachers, the shift in Catholic population to the suburbs and to public education. Some of the original reasons for Catholic schools in the city have vanished with the abolition of Bible readings in school. Catholic schools often use the same textbooks and materials as public schools in the standard academic subjects. Some groups are redefining Catholic education in the city to serve the poor and minority groups but at the same time many inner-city parishes have been consolidated.

Between 1970 and 1980 as many as 15,000 additional children may attend the Boston public schools as a result of the closing of parochial schools. The 30 new schools being planned in Boston are designed largely to replace nineteenth-century school structures, not to accommodate a 15 percent increase in school population.

Boston needs several kinds of help:

• Financial and educational information from pastors and diocesan officials about possible and actual plans to close parochial schools
• Emergency funds to lease facilities, either the abandoned school buildings or other nearby structures, and to finance whatever immediate repairs are necessary
• Contingency plans for both gradual and sudden increases in school enrollments, depending on state action concerning nonpublic schools

In Boston, the EPC should continue to work on these plans. The Public Facilities Department can lease buildings and the School Engineering Department can make them suitable for use. But Boston, like other Massachusetts cities, needs help from the state.

First, the Archdiocese of Boston, its financial advisors, board of education, pastors, and planners should share with public school representatives information about personnel, financial, and educational plans and priorities.

Second, the Commonwealth of Massachusetts should make available aid for leasing and renovating suitable facilities in Boston and other cities where parochial schools close.

Third, the Boston School Department should collaborate with spokesmen for nonpublic schools in situations where the law permits, for example, the several titles of ESEA which provide for loan of books and mutual efforts to combat the effects of poverty. Boston can pioneer models of cooperation in such areas as: (1) innovative programs of day care and adult literacy for Spanish-speaking people; (2) shared facilities, especially in the use of spaces and equipment; and (3) employment of well-trained teachers committed to working with the poor and disadvantaged—as members of religious orders worked in Boston schools in 1969-70.

The Example of the Spanish-Speaking Child

Twenty-five hundred Puerto Ricans lived in Boston in 1960. The number soared beyond 30,000 Puerto Ricans and 5,000 or 10,000 Cubans in Boston by 1970. For many of these Bostonians, Spanish is not just the first language; it is the only language. Several recent studies show a high proportion of families speak only Spanish, even after many years in the United States. Since Puerto Ricans are, by birthright, U.S. citizens and move freely back and forth between the mainland and Puerto Rico, they are perhaps the first minority group for whom assimilation is not typical. The extreme mobility of the Puerto Rican population in Boston hampered the development of a strong ethnic community that could help newcomers adjust to urban life and a strange culture.

Public school systems seek to break down ethnic identity because of the misguided notion that to be American means to conform to a single cultural type. Unfortunately, educators have not realized that by tearing away a child from the values and customs of his parents, they are not assuring his acceptance in the larger majority culture.

The schools make it almost impossible for non-English-speaking children to learn. Studies of Puerto Rican children in schools in New York City and Hawaii have found them well *below* average in both English and Spanish, and indeed in any skill requiring verbal comprehension. Preschool Puerto Rican children in the same places, however, score above average on tests of verbal skill in Spanish. Some educators have suggested that schooling in English may discourage verbal development in both languages. A student naturally learns to read and write in his native tongue, before he can master a second language. Bilingual education centers and Spanish collections in libraries such as Bibliotica Latina in the South End attempt to provide opportunities for development of a student's native language.

In typical schools, Puerto Rican children develop a strong consciousness of themselves as Puerto Ricans and as members of a particular social group. They quickly learn that they are different from North Americans. And then speaking Spanish becomes an act of defiance toward the authority of the school, and speaking English an act of submission—as well as an occasion for embarassment.

Few teachers, administrators, or counselors speak Spanish; even fewer speak it as their native language. The absentee and nonenrollment rates for Puerto Rican children are high. Too many who work with Spanish-speaking children agree with the teacher of English as a second language who told a member of the study staff, "Puerto Rican children just can't learn."

Boston community leaders estimate that between 5,000 and 10,000 Spanish-speaking children are of school age, but only 2,500 were enrolled in school in 1969, and just 250 of these were in senior high schools. Fewer than ten Spanish-speaking students graduated from Boston high schools in June 1970. Demographic factors account for some of the concentration at the lower grade levels, but a walk through any of ten Boston neighborhoods during school hours would reveal that thousands of older boys and girls, Spanish-speaking and others, have found nothing to attract or hold them in school.

In Boston, new teaching approaches must build on the strengths that Spanish-speaking children bring to school. Children and their parents must realize that they are valued in the community and the larger society. The school department must vigorously recruit teachers and other staff members with the skills and personal qualities necessary to meet the needs of Spanish-speaking children.

School officials have responded to the challenge that Spanish-speaking children pose in many ways. An assistant superintendent has had responsibility for programs for non-English-speaking children. These programs involve almost forty teachers of English as a second language (who work with children away from their regular classes), the Title VII Bilingual Program, and the English Language Center (formerly the Day School for Immigrants). A Boston teacher, coordinator of Title VII in the city, has been active in getting the program under way. Individual teachers and administrators have tried new approaches to meeting the needs of the Spanish-speaking child.

A program of "Transitional Bilingual Clusters" developed by leaders of the Spanish-speaking community, the staff of the Educational Development Center, and Boston School Department personnel, was supported unanimously by the school committee at meetings on August 20, October 14, and December 23, 1969. The program was introduced in January 1970 in Dorchester and the South End.

On February 10, 1970, the school committee established a Department of Bilingual Education to coordinate programs and services for children whose native language is not English. Other key appointments provide for a bilingual school and related services.

Despite this promising start, much remains to be done. Other school systems that made similar efforts decades ago are still struggling to produce significant results for Spanish-speaking children. There will be no easy solution in Boston, but the State Bilingual Education Act of 1971 offers state assistance to finance the Boston effort.

Problems and Recommendations. No one in the school department, the Spanish community, or any agency knows how many Spanish-speaking children of school age now live in Boston, nor how many to expect in a year. Studies based on a random sample of Spanish-speaking families have yielded valuable information about the characteristics of the Spanish community. But a head count is needed to determine how many children must be served. A continuing survey of neighborhoods is needed to keep pace with the mobility of many Spanish-speaking families and to assure that those who speak no English are not overlooked. All agencies that provide services to non-English-speaking people, including the school department, are responsible for conducting such surveys. Similar data is needed about the size of other non-English-speaking groups.

Recommendations

- The Boston School Department, the Department of Health and Hospitals, and other relevant public agencies must conduct annual surveys of neighborhoods in which sizable concentrations of non-English-speaking people may live. Surveys should be coordinated by a jointly-financed survey office.
- These surveys should be conducted during the summer, so Boston teachers and administrators with competence in the relevant language have the opportunity to participate in the surveys. Participation should be considered part of their in-service training.
- Teenagers from communities being surveyed should be employed in the summer to canvas. Community-based organizations should also have a major part in planning and executing the summer surveys.

Many Spanish-speaking children are never registered in school, and many others are never reregistered when their families move around Boston or back and forth to Puerto Rico, Miami, or New York City. School officials must deal sympathetically with the reasons for nonattendance—the essentially rural background of many families, limited parental education, lack of information on how to register children, lack of money for school lunches and clothing, and shyness in discussion with English-speaking Boston officials. Further, some children cannot find their way to school and many children report that other children, black and white, harass and tease them. Recently, only 50 children of the 1,170 enrolled in Headstart were Spanish-speaking. Boston has no attendance officers fluent in Spanish, nor many school secretaries trained to deal with Spanish-speaking parents.

Recommendations

- A Spanish-speaking registrar-secretary should be employed in each elementary district in which at least twenty Spanish-speaking families have been identified. The registrar-secretary should serve as a translator for conversations and for written materials. Parents should feel free to ask the registrar-secretary for help in making telephone calls to other agencies and for translation.

- All report cards, letters, and other communications to parents should be made available in Spanish and English. Materials should be prepared to orient Spanish-speaking parents to the Boston schools. Boston has already published "Your Child Begins School" in Spanish and should continue this practice for other publications.

- Teachers of Spanish-speaking children must be able to communicate with children in their native language and show respect for their foreign culture. Some teachers should be native Spanish-speakers. Unfortunately, the supply of certified Puerto Rican teachers is limited even in Puerto Rico, and teachers from other Latin American countries, including Cuba, are generally neither U.S. citizens nor eligible for certification to teach in Massachusetts.

Other city agencies have hired Puerto Ricans for community service and human relations work. There are three possible solutions: (1) advertise vigorously for native Spanish-speaking professionals; (2) negotiate with the state for special waivers to certify Spanish-speaking teachers who are not U.S. citizens; or (3) hire community people as teachers' aides to help in Spanish-speaking classrooms and encourage them to train for teaching positions.

A Boston area university could offer a certification program for native Spanish speakers who are often more effective teachers than college graduates with minors in Spanish.

Recommendations

- The organization of instruction in bilingual programs should allow auxiliary staff recruited from the Spanish-speaking community to have a major role in working with children. This role must not be limited to clerical and indirect services; it should include opportunity to relate to children in a way which shows that Spanish-speaking people are highly valued and trusted in the Boston schools.

- Auxiliary staff should work on annual contract, with full job security after a probationary period. Ability to speak fluent Spanish should be given significant weight in employing and promoting certified teachers.

- Materials for instruction in many subjects must be in Spanish. Also a variety of approaches should be developed to teach the Spanish-speaking child.

- Materials used in other cities to teach Spanish-speaking children should be reviewed. A committee with representatives from the Boston School Department and from the Spanish Federation should recommend materials to be adapted for use in Boston schools.

- In-service workshops should be conducted each year to discuss and evaluate new techniques and approaches. Rewards should be given for development of creative programs that meet needs of Spanish-speaking children.

- Standardized tests in English should not be given to children who speak a language other than English at home, until they have demonstrated a mastery of the English language in their school work.

The school must move closer to the Spanish-speaking child and his family. The school department proposal for cluster schools near neighborhoods and families deserves support. Clusters should be connected to large heterogeneous school facilities so children can be eased gradually into a more challenging environment.

Recommendations

- Bilingual programs for Spanish-speaking and other non-English-speaking children should be conducted in small facilities, including rented storefronts and underutilized public buildings. These programs should be linked to regular school programs to allow flexible movement of students as their language skills and self-confidence develop. The work-study program should expand to provide occupational opportunities for teenage Spanish-speaking students.
- A bilingual pupil adjustment counselor should be assigned to each elementary district in which at least twenty families have been identified who speak Spanish at home.

Note

1. See A STUDY OF PROMOTIONAL POLICIES AND PROCEDURES IN THE BOSTON PUBLIC SCHOOLS by Vincent C. Nuccio and Richard J. Doyle, April, 1970.

7

The Nonacademic Staff

The nonacademic staff of the Boston School Department is composed of those school employees who are support staff for teachers and administrators. With the exception of health service personnel (discussed· in another section), all are Civil Service personnel—school secretaries, attendance supervisors, attendance supervisors, cafeteria workers and custodians.

Many problems exist in recruiting, training, and coordinating nonacademic personnel. These problems will be intensified in the near future when expansion and change in some of the nonacademic departments take place. The school committee itself is presently directly responsible for the hiring of nonacademic staff. It devotes a major portion of its time to this—time which would be more profitably spent on matters relating directly to educational policy.

In recruiting, there is a great need in the system for working with the Civil Service Commission to schedule regular exams, to arrange walk-in exams when specific personnel shortages occur and to better advertise the positions available. The school department must recruit minority group personnel and interest them in the positions that exist. The school department, one of the largest employers of Civil Service personnel, has not made any attempt to coordinate its manpower needs with the Civil Service Commission.

Training nonacademic personnel is disorganized and uncoordinated. Training manuals exist for some jobs (e.g., custodians), but not for others (e.g., cafeteria workers). Secretaries must be trained to use new office machines and custodians must learn to care for modern building materials and new facilities. Secretaries, custodians, carefeteria personnel, and attendance supervisors are isolated within a school, even though they serve the same children.

Present grievance procedures are complex and different for each department. All serious grievances go to the school committee which is already too busy with details of personnel management.

The system of filling vacancies and transferring personnel is unnecessarily complicated and ineffective, because of Civil Service regulations and the school department's own procedures. For example, a city hospital kitchen worker cannot transfer to a school kitchen without a new exam; an assistant cafeteria manager from another Massachusetts city is barred from a comparable position in Boston because of residency requirements. The range of promotional possibilities is small, and in most cases, it is nearly impossible to make lateral transfers. When such transfers are possible, as with secretaries, the system is at the mercy of the transferee who retains complete tenure and seniority and has the right to stay where she wants for as long as she wants.

97

No general pattern of supervision or decentralization within the city applies to all school personnel. Presently, thirty-six attendance districts coincide neither with school districts nor areas; they are based on an old geographic formula and the intensity of attendance problems. Five custodial districts are under the jurisdiction of the deputy and assistant schoolhouse custodians. Thirty-seven cafeteria managers (as of 1970) are spread out at schools throughout the city.

No systematic means for evaluating nonacademic personnel exist. Nor are there performance standards for each position. The position of supervisor of nonacademic personnel should be created. The supervisor would work under and be responsible to the associate superintendent for personnel and would be in charge of all personnel matters for custodians, secretaries, attendance supervisors, cafeteria staff, and health service personnel. He would coordinate recruiting, vacancies and transfers, review of grievances, training, and nominating.

The supervisor of nonacademic personnel would coordinate with the Civil Service Commission in scheduling exams. He would work to recruit minority group personnel by developing joint programs with such agencies as ABCD and its neighborhood APACs, and the Mayor's Office of Human Rights to educate and interest people in the employment opportunities offered by the school department. The supervisor of nonacademic personnel would also be able to oversee all training programs for nonacademic staff.

Chapter 208, of the acts of 1965 should be changed so that the superintendent, on the recommendation of the associate superintendent for personnel, would have the authority to nominate the nonacademic staff.

Grievance procecures should not be handled by the school committee. A uniform grievance plan, similar to the four-step procedure used by employees, should be adopted.

The supervisor of nonacademic personnel should attempt to coordinate the boundaries of the districts of the nonacademic departments to eliminate overlapping and minimize confusion. He should work with the directors of the nonacademic departments to establish new districts, eventually to coincide with the area superintendents' districts.

The supervisor should work with department heads to establish evaluative criteria for each position and to see that evaluations are systematically carried out. There should be promotion possibilities for qualified workers and safeguards to prevent promoting incompetent workers on a seniority basis.

Supervisors of Attendance

All children of school age are required to attend school unless they are specifically exempted by the superintendent. Attendance supervisors have two functions: t.e child advocacy function, which says the right of children to attend school must be protected and the policing function which says the law requiring their attendance must be enforced.

There are now two heads of the Department of Attendance (after a tie score, the committee named both candidates!), a coordinator, and forty-one attendance supervisors. District boundaries are based on the number of school-age children, plus the number of attendance cases in specific geographic areas of the city. These geographic areas do not coincide with school districts. Some schools are on the regular rounds of two or more attendance supervisors, while others are not on anyone's regular rounds. The office keeps detailed but not very adequate records, and the investigations (each phone call or visit counts as one investigation) it makes are tallied. Fewer than 1 percent of the total number of investigations result in court cases. They find truancy in about 10 percent of the investigations.

The total number of investigations is really not an evaluation of the department's accomplishments. As the number of investigations increases each year, it seems to indicate a failure on the part of the schools to keep children interested in attending school.

The population of the city is changing, and many of the newer inhabitants have a different attitude towards school than did their predecessors. Communication with non-English-speaking people is a problem. The attendance department has made attempts to respond to this problem by in-service Spanish language lessons, a mental health program with Harvard Medical School, and adding attendance supervisors in high truancy areas. These measures seem sensible but they have not yet stopped the increase in truancy.

Another crucial problem attendance supervisors face is that they are responsible for the entire process of getting and keeping children in school. For example, the attendance supervisor presumably must make a diagnosis (this child needs emotional help; this child does not have winter clothes for school) confer with teachers and principals, and in a case of established truancy, follow through with court proceedings and the child's possible assignment to a county training school. In short, he is asked to function simultaneously as a counselor and a policeman which is often too much to expect.

The supervisor is asked to have skill in investigation, social work, coordination, and law. The department of attendance has suggested that a bachelor's degree and training in social work become requisites for obtaining a position in the department. Currently, almost all of the supervisors are former police officers with little formal training. The head supervisors also support the MACE recommendation made that attendance should be a function of an enlarged pupil services department. In the past, the department of attendance has been under the jurisdiction of the associate superintendent for junior highs. The school department has already begun planning for a unified special services department under the jurisdiction of an associate superintendent for special services. Members of the attendance department like to see themselves as providing guidance for wayward children. They feel that the public sees them only as truant officers and their role as defined by law reinforces this image. Unfortunately, most attendance supervisors describe their jobs in terms of court proceedings and the need to keep parents and children in line.

Recommendations

- Teams of special service personnel, including a limited number of attendance supervisors, should be assigned to each of the six school areas. A detailed proposal for this is in the section on the special services.
- Instead of expecting one person to play two conflicting roles—child advocacy and truancy prevention—the study team recommends that attendance supervisors be divided into two groups: (1) Police Officers who would conduct the census of school-age children and enforce the compulsory attendance law in its legal and punitive aspects, serving warrants and following through with court proceedings; and (2) Child Advocates who would work to protect the rights of children, work closely with the pupil adjustment counselors, and who would be the field personnel for the special services team in their area.
- Attendance supervisors should be specially qualified in law or in the field of juvenile investigation. Child advocates should have a college degree with concentration in psychology or social work and experience in school guidance, social work, or in a public or private health or welfare agency.
- The ratio of child advocates to officers should be three to one in the next ten years. A relatively low number of the investigations (about 10 percent of the total) result in established truancy. The ratio would vary depending on a district's needs.
- To change the structure of the department with a minimum of confusion, the study staff recommends that officers be paid at the current salary, or be allowed to transfer to other city departments, like the probation officers, at the same salary. Child advocates should be put on the teacher salary scale, although most of them should work on cases before and after school hours and may need to work on a year-round basis eventually.

School Secretaries

The school secretary in Boston keeps the school office running smoothly, handles everyday communications, regulates the flow of information from the outside into the school and from the school to the outside. Much of her job deals with communication and public relations. She is a coordinator between the principal and other members of his staff (e.g., she notifies people about meetings and makes appointments) and between the schoolhouse and other departments within the system (e.g., nurses, attendance supervisors, and central school headquarters).

An estimated 60 percent of the secretary's duties involve dealing with people. However, secretaries do not now receive any training in communication and public relations skills. Secretaries concentrate on protecting the principal from outside intrusions, rather than facilitating communication between the principal and others.

Particularly in neighborhoods that are changing, secretaries, who are often the first contact between the school and the community, must learn to deal effectively and sympathetically with new and old families in the community. Because the secretary is the principal's representative she must understand his position in various matters to effectively channel communications to him. Some secretaries are aware of these problems and are rated excellent by their principals; others must improve.

Recommendations

- The school department must focus more on public relations qualifications when it recruits and selects school secretaries. Now, no formal job standards exist beyond standard civil service requirements. Supervisors of nonacademic personnel should develop these standards.
- The school department should develop in-service training programs to help school secretaries communicate more effectively. The department should take advantage of the free training courses the New England Telephone Company offers to teach on the art of telephone public relations. Also, the school department should investigate the possibility of providing sensitivity training for secretaries. Courses to help them deal with minority groups and the poor are taught at the Human Relations Center at Boston University and elsewhere.
- Principals and central office administrators should be able to interview at least three candidates for a secretarial position and to accept them on a three month trial or probationary period.

Cafeteria Workers

Pending state legislation requires that all school systems in Massachusetts have the capacity to feed all their pupils.

The school lunch program has already changed because of political pressure. For example, the bag lunch program, originally part of the federally-sponsored Operation Counterpoise, was intended to provide adequate nutrition to children from disadvantaged homes. Until this program began, parents never expected the schools to feed their children. Problems arose when parents of children who did not receive lunch began to feel that their children were being cheated. Because of the problems of expansion the school committee has voted against receiving state money for the lunch program. Even with state and federal funding, the programs are a financial burden on the school system. At the same time, they require a large amount of new paperwork. And now, there is increasing pressure to provide breakfasts as well as lunches.

The Boston School Committee at first turned down comprehensive central kitchen plans which would make hot meals available for all children. The patch-work arrangement they eventually accepted may reach as few as 40 percent, despite increased federal aid.

If the Boston schools will not provide hot meals, it is only reasonable for the state to authorize other Boston neighborhood agencies, community development corporations, or other centers to use the funds earmarked for Boston children. New York City parents have already asked for community-run school lunch programs. It is unjust that so many suburban school children benefit from federally-aided school lunch programs while so many Boston children lack even the option of a hot lunch.

These anticipated changes will affect cafeteria staffing. As of 1970, 39 of Boston's 193 schools had cafeterias, and children in 11 other schools were fed with the bag lunch system. A central kitchen to serve 29 outlying schools would require installing heating and refrigeration units and serving equipment in each building. Under the central kitchen program, planning staff at central head-quarters, production staff in the central kitchen, staff involved in trucking and delivery, and part-time cafeteria staff in the individual schools will be necessary.

The variety of lunch programs that now exists is a result of adaptation to existing conditions. The present school lunch department staff cannot make future projections and plans for expansion. The central office needs new personnel who are skilled in planning. Because much of the expansion is required by legislation, the state should be responsible for helping Boston establish a new lunch program. Two people from the State Department of Education, School Lunch Division, are working with the system. Also, the state has provided $400,000 to equip the central kitchen facility. But the school system will need additional personnel and funds.

Great help is needed for future planning. First, the lunch department should be placed under the business manager's jurisdiction. Full-time people who can do statistical analysis and forecasting must be hired or outside experts consulted. Planners should present and discuss alternative models for expansion. Perhaps the system should plan to contract with any of a number of business firms who might provide staff and food on an area basis, as do many private firms and agencies. It is doubtful that the city school department could provide the most efficient food service. The Educational Planning Center, perhaps with help from the Boston Finance Commission or Municipal Research Bureau, should consult representatives of state and federal agencies and private firms to secure estimates and eventually bids on a food service system. If Boston is to switch to a totally centralized kitchen, it must decide to contract for part of the food to be prepared by an outside firm or to prepare all the food itself. If officials choose not to contract with outside firms for preparation, they must consider whether to contract with a trucking firm for delivery and unloading or to build this capacity into the system and hire many new workers.

Custodians

Custodians hold an important and responsible position in the school system. Boston parents desire good school facilities for their children, and school officials like to boast the best-run and best-equipped buildings. The beginning salary for a custodian is close to that of a beginning teacher and can rise to over $10,000 a year. In spite of this, custodians are made to feel inadequate and are isolated from the rest of the system.

Custodians are considered only janitors by the public, teachers, and school officials. When costs were trimmed in the construction of the new Trotter School, the first space to be eliminated was the custodians' room. Recruiting is a problem because, despite high salaries, the janitor image does not appeal to responsible young men, especially those of minority groups who are anxious to escape from job categories they consider menial. Drinking has been a problem with some custodians. The Chief Schoolhouse Custodian, whose title should be changed to director of plant maintenance, has been unable to change the image of the custodian's job, although he continues to work on this problem. Standards can be (and have been) set and recommendations can be made, but nothing will change if the public, school officials, and custodians maintain their present attitudes.

The custodians are a tight knit group isolated from the rest of the system. They are not part of state or nationwide groups. They lobby independently of the rest of the school system and very effectively most of the time. Proposals for a new training program met with resistance from both the school committee and the custodians' association. The school committee would like to provide jobs for constituents, and it is presently involved in appointing custodians and handling grievances—functions that should be handled by the schoolhouse custodian who has knowledge and skill in these areas. The custodians are most interested in keeping their jobs. The 1944 Strayer report and the 1955 Jacobs survey recommended changes in the custodian's position; however, few changes have occurred. The present schoolhouse custodian has been studying problems, setting standards, and making recommendations. But both the custodian's image and the organizational structure must change if any progress is to be made.

At present, the custodians' association and the school committee have more power over programs and policies than does the schoolhouse custodian. And the problem will intensify soon. With passage of the antiair-pollution bond, which provides Boston with $1,600,000 to convert coal furnaces to gas or oil, fewer custodians will be needed in some buildings. Eighteen furnaces have already been replaced, changing staffing requirements and requiring new skills and responsibilities in several schools.

Recommendations

- The school committee should not be involved in personnel matters involving custodians. Instead, it should work with the schoolhouse custodian to upgrade the image of the custodian. The Boston School Department, the Custodians Association, the Civil Service Commission, and community agencies (e.g., ABCD) should collaborate to promote and project the role of the school custodian as the protector of the school plant, and to recruit young men into careers as custodians. In individual schools, the school department should develop a program introducing and explaining the job of the custodian (perhaps similar to the program on policemen). Also, the school department should provide handsomely designed uniforms for custodians, such as those worn by airline technical personnel.
- The schoolhouse custodian should have the responsibility and authority to make decisions regarding his staff as long as his plans do not conflict with systemwide goals. His title should be changed to director of plant maintenance. He should be able to implement training programs and with school department support, make necessary changes. And he should be provided a budget for training his staff and implementing changes, rather than having change thrust upon him by the school committee. Where it is possible, the school department should provide leaves of absence to train custodians in new maintenance techniques and materials as the schoolhouse custodian recommends.
- The director of plant maintenance and the supervisor of nonacademic personnel should establish new staffing standards.
- The school department should assure the custodians association that no competent man will lose his job because of a change in staffing standards. Politics must be kept out of the system. The association should agree to the phasing out of unnecessary jobs with assurance that the city or school department will provide retraining.

Vocational Education

Untrained men and women are frequently unemployed and thus contribute to the nation's growing welfare costs. At the same time, trained workers who can fill the needs of today's technological society are in great demand.

American educators are realizing that the traditional "college preparatory" curriculum is unsuited to the interests and needs of many individuals. For a large number of students, vocational education that teaches general skills needed for a particular occupation is more valuable. In response to the growing need for trained workers, the federal Vocational Education Act of 1963 has provided millions of dollars annually to support occupational education. Massachusetts has recently planned a number of new vocational-technical schools.

The trade schools, Boston High, the business curriculum in most comprehensive high schools, and the industrial arts, cooperative and distributive education programs in Boston schools attempt to teach occupational skills to students.

Surveys of occupational trends indicate a movement away from agriculture and industry toward the service field with increasing emphasis on human care (health, education, and other social services for all income levels). A second change is in the stability of a given job; as technology changes equipment and the nature of work, a worker may need retraining six or more times during his or her lifetime. A narrow vocational skill emphasis (e.g., on the internal combustion engine or the platen press) is no longer appropriate; even the content of shop math or related English must provide bases for students' later needs.

Boston's programs in vocational education reflect not only the philosophy of another era, but also the economics of the 1920s and 1930s. The Vocational Education Program depends on the "Trade and Industry" approach developed in the World War I era. Young men and women are trained for fields that are stable or declining—such as agriculture or machine work in factories soon to be automated or closed.

Some programs in Boston provide relevant skills and job opportunities. For more than fifty years distributive education (marketing, merchandising) with the Board of Retail Trade has provided limited November to January on-the-job training in Boston department stores. The Licensed Practical Nurses Program has graduated more than 500 young women while most school systems were unconcerned about the nursing shortage. Boston offers programs in central and area high schools to train much-needed plumbers, electricians, auto mechanics and auto body repairmen. These programs should be maintained and expanded.

The program in Jamaica Plain High School, which includes work oppor-

Table 8-1
Students Enrolled in Vocational Courses 1969-70

Boston Trade High School	635
Trade High School for Girls	317
Cooperative Industrial Courses	
Boston Technical High	173
Brighton High	303
Charlestown High	396
Dorchester High	215
East Boston High	129
Hyde Park High	159
South Boston High	145
Agriculture Course—Jamaica Plain High	88
Boston Vocational Technical Institute	89
Boston High School (Work-Study)	418

tunities in Woburn (an interesting use of Metropolitan area resources—a garden and floral center), should also be maintained. The Boston Board of Superintendents has begun to redefine the program away from traditional agriculture (crops and animal husbandry) towards horticulture. Boston will need men and women trained to care for its world famous Public Gardens, the Fenway, Olmstead Park, many cemetaries and the Arnold Arboretum. New programs in health careers, data processing, technical information services, and accelerated science and technology are badly needed.

In Boston, there are four directors of separate education departments for occupational education. Careers in business (secretarial and clerical), are separated from careers in merchandising (buying and selling) although both are branches of business. Vocational education officials are concerned with trades and industry. Home economics focuses on nutrition and foods. It includes sewing and dress design but neither selling clothes (distributive education) nor textile production (vocational education). Existing departments reflect the philosophy and labels of the first third of the century.

The Department of Occupational Education should be reorganized to coordinate vocational education, business education, distributive education, home economics, and probably industrial arts. Present directors would remain as assistant directors under the direction of an individual from outside the system who has had experience in developing new occupational and technical programs, cooperating with personnel in the growing fields of health, science, and research information. This director might be an assistant superintendent for both adult and vocational education, which involve work with state and federal officials to plan manpower and occupational programs. He would need an assistant director (screened as the dean's study suggests).

In 1969 $5.75 million in federal funds were channeled to occupational education programs in Massachusetts; only $35,350 went to the Boston Public Schools. Although Boston has over 7 percent of the public school students in the state, the city received less than 1 percent of these federal funds. The primary reason for this was the school department's failure to submit proposals for funding. For example, in Massachusetts almost a million dollars in federal money (15 percent of the total state allocation) is available to develop vocational education programs for the disadvantaged. However, the Boston School Department did not submit a proposal to fund a training program for students from economically disadvantaged homes until 1970. The state allocation to Boston rose sharply in 1971 and 1972 as part of the response to this report.

When budget allocations are made, vocational education will always compete with other educational programs. But allocation problems must be resolved by adherence to rationally developed, clearly articulated priorities, rather than by reference to existing programs and last year's budget. The 1968 Massachusetts Advisory Council of Education study, OCCUPATIONAL EDUCATION FOR MASSACHUSETTS, concluded that too large a percentage of school funds is spent on the general and college preparatory curricula and that more must be allocated to vocational education. This conclusion is especially true in Boston.

The closing of one trade school and efforts to expand programs at Boston High are indications that the vocational education system in Boston is not totally unchanging. Yet, overall efforts in vocational education are timid, unimaginative, and likely to continue past programs rather than develop new ones. Too often the schools have justified inaction by citing reasons why a new idea will not work. For example, educators complain that parents and students prefer the general or college-preparatory curricula; they do not enroll in vocation education programs. A far more significant reason has been the schools' failure to develop exciting vocational opportunities and publicize them aggressively. In another case, directors explained that headmasters can prevent new vocational education programs from being introduced in their schools. Often this has little to do with the program's merits or the students' needs but rather with the headmaster's unwillingness to accept new ideas or open "his" school to other groups in the city. Fortunately, several headmasters actively support new programs.

The MACE Study, OCCUPATIONAL EDUCATION FOR MASSACHU-SETTS, contains an excellent analysis of vocational education and its place in the curriculum. Many of its recommendations should stimulate the Boston schools' efforts in vocational education and the school department must consider them.

A new Department of Occupational Education should be formed to plan and prepare a program for all Boston children in occupational-technical-vocational skills. The major emphasis for a three-to-five-year period would be on planning and developing new programs in health, science, and services careers—for children and adults. Two health occupation programs are currently being planned. The directors of vocational education, business education, distributive education, and industrial arts should be designated as assistant directors of this department. The director shall be recruited from a position of proven leadership in another local system or state agency concerned with manpower and educational development.

Those concerned with vocational education in Boston should visit exemplary vocational programs throughout the state and nation (such as Pittsburgh) on the advice of state and federal consultants. Educational planners in Boston must place high priority on updating the vocational education program and on projecting staff and facilities requirements for the future.

Plans for the Occupational Resource Center, a new school for vocational education, have existed for several years. Delays are intolerable because the center is needed and building costs are rising at the rate of $200,000 per month for a school of this size. Regional vocational/technical schools of comparable size have been planned and built in Massachusetts communities within a two-year period.

The headmaster who will administer the ORC during the first years ought to head the planning effort. He must have demonstrated capacities for developing new, exciting vocational education programs.

The school department should develop a firm time table for the planning, construction and opening of the Occupational Resource Center. The department should settle on a site as soon as possible since that decision will greatly influence the ORC's development.

Chapter 74 of the General Laws of Massachusetts provides that the state will reimburse any community for 50 percent of the net maintenance costs of vocational education programs. However, this money is deposited in the general fund of the responsible institutions—in this case, the Boston city government—it is not earmarked specifically for vocational education. The Massachusetts legislature should amend chapter 74 so that money which is dispensed to Boston under the law is restricted to the vocational education program for which it is intended.

Staff from Boston's schools and medical community must work together to develop vocational education programs in health careers for high school students. Boston is one of the nation's leading medical centers. As medical services expand, the need for skilled men and women grows. By 1975 it is expected that health care will be the nation's largest industry, employing one out of every sixteen persons.

Dean Ammer of Northeastern University in 1970 completed a study which revealed 5,000 unfilled job openings in the Boston metropolitan area for workers trained in a variety of health occupations. Similar shortages exist on a national level. At this time, no vocational education opportunities in health careers exist for Boston high school students, although a limited program to train practical nurses and dental assistants is offered at the post graduate level (grades 13 and 14) at Girl's Trade.

Consequently, on January 28th, 1970 the school study staff brought together persons from the schools and hospitals to discuss its recommendation that opportunities in health careers be developed. The school department later assumed primary responsibility for development and submitted a proposal to the Department of Education for funding a program in health careers. This is a first step, but the city may also need to commit its own funds to secure state and federal grants.

Recommendations

- During the next few years the school department should develop and offer introductory courses in health careers and health skills in selected high schools, beginning courses in the ninth grade. In later years, students should have opportunities to expand their knowledge and train for specific jobs in health fields.
- Schools should use the Health Vocational Training Center at the New England Hospital in Roxbury as a training site. Federal funds for programs for the disadvantaged could support the effort, and by using the site, the schools would not have to purchase the expensive equipment that might be needed if all health training were done in high schools. The department should also explore the possible use of the Training Center for Comprehensive Care at the Lemuel Shattuck Hospital and hospitals for the clinical component of training.
- The success of this program will depend greatly on the appointment of a highly qualified health careers coordinator and on the cooperation between the schools and advisors from the medical community.
- Guidance counselors, guidance advisers, principals and headmasters should learn about career opportunities in the health services field. Students beginning junior high school should be able to learn about various kinds of nursing and technical jobs (therapists, technicians, dieticians) in the health field. Educators should also seek to eliminate rigid barriers in the health profession. These barriers, which in many cases prevent mobility from one job level to the next, exist primarily because of licensing regulations and training requirements.

What applies to training for careers in health also applies to careers in data-processing. Educators must master basic data-processing information for their own purposes and for counseling children.

The study staff investigated in detail the work-study program originally planned to reach potential dropouts and subsequently financed under Title I, ESEA and other sources. The program is related principally to occupational education; Boston High School has developed productive relationships with more than fifty employers. The success of work-study comes from thorough planning, careful selection of staff, and constant liaison with employers and students' families. The Boston High School program now serves more than 400 students; it should be expanded to serve 1,200 students and eventually 2,000 or more.

Boston High School officials have already acknowledged problems of expansion and minority employment opportunity. Officials know they must reach Spanish-speaking families. They must include a bilingual approach for Spanish families who may question whether high school study is necessary or relevant. One work-study center might be based in Roxbury to emphasize jobs in small business firms. Also, the work-study approach should be adapted to the hours and needs of hospital and health centers in all parts of the city.

Expansion could begin immediately, but it must be planned as part of the occupational education program. The in-school program must provide not only basic education but also some specialty courses required for jobs above the low-entry minimum skill level. Provision for the return of one-time truants to other high schools and the ORC must be carefully planned. The system could eventually support separate, parallel and even competitive programs to give career-oriented students maximum choice.

To improve the work-study program:

- The school department, using federal, state and city funds, should expand the work-study program first—to 1,200 and eventually to 2,000 or more high school students.
- Planning efforts must include employers, communities, and families. The program should respond especially to inner-city youth, but should include occupational opportunities in all sections of the metropolitan area (e.g., Everett, Cambridge, Route 128).
- Students over fourteen years old with a history of attendance problems should be encouraged to enroll in the program.

School Health Programs

School health programs for Boston children can be divided into three parts: health education, environmental health, and personal health services. Personal health services are further divided into three parts: dental, medical and psychological.

- The health education department instructs students in proper health habits and personal hygiene. (Department of Physical Education and Health Education.)
- The environmental health department protects and promotes the health of the school community. (Department of Safety.)
- The personal health services department attempts to prevent, detect, and correct conditions which may impair a student's ability to learn. (Dental and medical: Department of School Health Services; psychological: Department of Pupil Adjustment Counseling.)

In addition special schools (Horace Mann for the Deaf) and departments provide instruction for students with unusual emotional, physical and mental needs.

The departments for students with unusual problems are: classes for the emotionally disturbed; instruction of physically handicapped; perceptually handicapped; speech and hearing; special classes; and vision resources. These departments should share a common boundary within the organization of the schools. Presently, however, health services and educational efforts for those with special physical and emotional needs are placed randomly in the Boston school's organization. School health services until 1970 were under the associate superintendent for junior high school education. Health education was under the associate superintendent for high school education. The other departments were under the associate superintendent for special services.

The Department of School Health Services (DSHS)

Of all the departments concerned with school health and education for students with special needs, the school study staff examined the Department of School Health Services most extensively.

111

Administration

The administrative structure of the DSHS has remained essentially unchanged for twenty-five years. The DSHS was under the auspices of the Associate Superintendent for Junior High Schools, but the department enjoys much administrative autonomy.

However, any major change in the operations of the DSHS is subject to the formal approval by the Board of Superintendents. The Boston School Committee may be involved in alterations of personnel requirements or in any major program changes.

Personnel

The DSHS as of 1970 employed fifty-four permanent school physicians and five temporary physicians. Most of the doctors are in their fifties or sixties; a few are younger; one part-timer is seventy-eight. Only one is a pediatrician. Usually, each physician covers three to five schools; he is expected to spend an average of ten hours each week on school health.

The average annual salary of permanent school physicians is $5,500 for annual physical examinations and daily visits to each school. The school department has requested civil service to grant "open and unassembled" examinations for prospective school physicians. In effect, this means, that future applicants will not have to take any examination at all.

The school nursing staff (1970) consists of seventy-five permanent nurses and eighteen temporary appointees. One nurse is assigned full-time to each of the seventeen high schools. The remaining permanent nurses are responsible for two to four (and in one case, five) elementary and junior high schools. The average pupil to permanent nurse ratio is about 1300:1.

Although permanent school nurses are not under civil service, they are tenured and salaried as school teachers are. The average permanent school nurse earns more than $9,100 a year. Turnover is low and the waiting list is long.

Programs

Physical Examinations. Massachusetts law requires that each child entering the public schools be examined by a doctor. The law stipulates that physical examinations must include a vision and hearing test (not necessarily by a doctor) and inspection of the feet. Beyond this, it provides that the Department of Public Health may determine the manner and intervals of additional examinations (MGLA Chap. 71 Sect. 57).

The current regulations for the physical examination of school children in Massachusetts require a physician to examine certain types of students.

The school committee regulation regarding health examinations states that every school child must be examined by a physician every year (Rules of the School Committee and Regulations of the Public Schools, Section 248).

The actual DSHS physical examination program provides more frequent examination than required by the public health regulations, but less frequent than officially required by the school committee. As required by the state law (MGLA Chap. 71 Sect. 56) and Public Health regulations (Para. 7), all defects and disabilities detected during the physical exams are reported to the child's parents.

Massachusetts Public Health Regulations require that every pupil's vision and hearing be tested annually (Para. 4). Nurses also measure the height and weight of every student once each year, as the Public Health Regulations (Para. 5) require.

Immunizations. Massachusetts law requires that all students entering schools be certified by a physician to be vaccinated against smallpox and immunized against diphtheria, pertusis, tetanus, measles and poliomyelitis (MGLA Chap. 76 Sect. 15).

Tuberculosis Case Finding. School nurses, with the City Department of Health and Hospitals, conduct a tuberculosis case-finding and referral service.

DSHS Budget

The DSHS budget for fiscal 1969 is $1,221,000. More than 96 percent of this money is earmarked for salaries. The total 1969 expenditures for all health purposes in the Boston Public Schools is estimated to be at least 2 million dollars. (The total 1969 Boston Public School budget for general school purposes exceeds $68 million.)

The school department must give increased attention and energy relying on neighborhood health clinics to provide for children's health needs; reviewing and, in some cases, changing DSHS programs and priorities; improving DSHS information and data collection system; and using the professional skills of school health personnel.

Neighborhood Health Clinics. Neighborhood health clinics such as the Roxbury Comprehensive Health Clinic, the Bunker Hill Health Center, and the Tufts-New England Clinic at Columbia Point, are becoming more common in Boston. City officials envision similar facilities in each of the economically disadvantaged areas, and a recent grant to Boston City Hospital will make possible a clinic in the South End.

Under the governor's 1970 plan, the number of neighborhood health centers could increase. Two centers opened in Boston during 1970. Clinics like these will bring health care close to families in their neighborhoods and often close to schools; educators must begin to rethink the assumptions underlying existing school health programs.

In the future, a neighborhood clinic may assume the responsibility for a child's health care as part of a prepaid family health insurance plan. When this happens, one must question the wisdom of parallel medical services provided by schools. Even now, the need for daily M.D. visits to all schools is a questionable use of medical time and talent.

Programs and Priorities. Current priorities and programs are:

- School health service personnel have identified dental problems as the most serious unmet health need among Boston school children. Few of the schools' or city's resources are devoted to meeting this problem.
- Over 1.2 million dollars are allocated annually to the DSHS. Their efforts are designed primarily to meet medical needs. The Department of Pupil Adjustment Counseling is allocated just over $400,000 to help students with emotional difficulties. Considering the emotional needs of many adolescents, the school department should reexamine the allocation of resources between physical and mental health needs.
- School health personnel and services should be distributed throughout the city on the basis of need. In lower income areas, medical resources are more limited and health needs are more likely to be unmet than in middle and upper income areas.
- The first preschool or K-I physical examination should be more thorough than any examination now given in the schools. If a diagnostic physical were given, health problems could be discovered and treated early. At the same time, school officials could determine which students do not need examinations as often as the school provides.

Information System. The school nurse spends about 50 percent of her time on school health records. The backbone of the health records system is the Work-Book which each nurse is asked to keep in the center drawer of her desk. Each nurse is also responsible for maintaining a neat, up-to-date, personal health record (#301) for each pupil. A nurse must record virtually everything she does, often twice or more. Nurses use more than five dozen official forms and reports. At the year's end, the DSHS Annual Statistical Report is published. This document supplements the department director's brief Annual Report to the Superintendent, which contains reflections on school health and a description of some of the department's programs.

The DSHS Annual Statistical Report is essentially a numerical chronicle of the department's activities and findings; it has no clear purpose. Many statistics in the report are of doubtful relevance. Some statistics are clearly worthless.

The existing DSHS information system fulfills certain legal requirements (notification of parents or the Public Health Department). Also, the system acts as an all-purpose reservoir, indiscriminately storing all the department's information. But besides being nonselective, the DSHS health information system is expensive, estimated to cost over $400,000 annually in personnel time alone.

Personnel. School nurses do many things only incidentally related to their training, such as keeping health records and transporting children to clinics. Moreover many of their present nursing functions, taking temperatures or treating cuts and bruises could be handled by less highly trained persons.

School doctors make daily calls to their schools, administer the schools' immunization programs and give physical examinations. The only one of these functions doctors must fulfill is giving physicals and these can be administered in health centers (or by family doctors) rather than in the schools. No longer is a school exam likely to be as comprehensive as one in a clinic or doctor's office with blood and urine tests. School nurses are fully qualified to give innoculations.

Recommendations

- The Superintendent should appoint a Health Advisory Board to work with the associate superintendent for special services responsible for health services. This board would be composed of professional persons representing a variety of public and private institutions in the health field.

  Many public and private agencies and institutions are concerned with providing and planning for Boston's health needs. The Health Advisory Board would bring the schools into contact with the greater medical community, reducing fragmentation of services, fostering coordination and communication, and involving the schools in the city's changing health services.

  Currently the schools' health services are supervised by several associate superintendents, the superintendent and the school committee. The Health Advisory Board would be better qualified to assist school health services establish priorities, operate effectively, and attain greater coordination between school and community health services.

- The job of school physician should be phased out and the school nurse or neighborhood health clinic should assume his responsibilities. Using clinic doctors makes it unnecessary for a child to see two doctors, one for screening and one for treatment. Moreover the health clinic is equipped to perform more thorough physical examinations than is possible in the school setting. If a clinic is unable to take over all the school doctor's functions, the schools should contract out for specific services, for example, routine physical exams. The daily school call can be eliminated.

- The Boston schools should provide more resources for psychological services, especially for high school students, concentrate on dental needs, and redistributing resources with respect to need.

  To begin solving the dental problem, the school department should consider staffing the unused dental facilities now available in several schools. Also, the DSHS should work with the newly appointed director of Boston's dental health program. Finally, Boston should consider implementing a preventive program similar to flouridation.

- The information collection and reporting system of the DSHS should be streamlined. A separate, detailed set of recommendations has been sent to the DSHS.

  At this time the DSHS does not use the school department-supported Department of Data Processing to better organize its information services. The statistics compiled by the DSHS should help allocate resources on the basis of need, identify trends in children's health and provide information on how effectively schools were correcting defects.

- The school department should explore ways to reduce the number of schools nurses and to employ health aides at considerable dollar savings. The aides at some schools should be bilingual.

  The school department should employ health aides in several schools to relieve the nurse of many of her routine or clerical functions. The school nurse's duties would need to be redefined so that they would correspond to her training as a Registered Nurse.

  The school department should experiment to determine the setting in which the school nurse can best function. Some school nurses should be located in neighborhood health centers rather than in school.

- Existing resources must be reallocated and, in some cases, new funds made available for changes to take place. The DSHS should consult the 1970 amendments to the Elementary and Secondary Education Act of 1965, specifically Title VII, Section 808. The act provides funds for a variety of projects to meet the health needs of low income children.

10 The Special Needs of Children

Boston pioneered in the creation of special learning opportunities for blind and deaf children. The system provided special classes as a need was demonstrated—classes for the retarded, for the physically or perceptually handicapped, and for the emotionally disturbed. Over the years, the school system has expanded these special services.

However, many organizational arrangements, personnel policies, and cooperative relationships have recently been questioned. Some parents have brought suit against the schools to guarantee certain rights to students in special classes. Moreover, the schools have been accused of ignoring the needs of many out-of-school youths.

In a 1969 report, a team of organizational analysts from M.I.T. pointed out some problems in the Special Services Department. They found no coordination between the several types of pupil services. Three separate associate superintendents had responsibility for related departments. The departments themselves were dispersed throughout the city. The school department, recognizing these problems, plans to consolidate the departments under one office.

Ineffective communication between many department heads in the special services area is a serious problem. Little vertical (i.e., between superior and subordinate) or horizontal (i.e., between department directors) communication takes place between staff members. A survey of staff indicated that about 89 percent of the directors report meeting with their superiors once a month or less frequently and 78 percent report meeting less than once a month. Directors of departments within special services report spending only about 11 percent of their time working with other directors of special services. They feel that they should be spending twice that amount engaged in this activity.

The M.I.T. study discovered that the information exchanged between the special services departments is generally of poor quality. The three man committee appointed to evaluate the Department of Pupil Adjustment Counseling found the Departments of Educational Investigation and Measurement, Attendance, and Pupil Adjustment Counseling overlap functionally but "work totally independently and without intercommunication." Some department directors even withhold needed information on children and their problems from other directors and claim that it would be "unprofessional" to share it.

Following is the rank order of resources which directors could choose to help them be more effective administrators in a school system:

Resource	Rank
More personnel	1
More time to develop programs	2
Information	3
More support from those in authority	4
More funds	5
More legal authority	6
More supplies	7
More influential friends in the system	8
More experience	9
An advanced university degree	10

The M.I.T. report also emphasized that many departmental directors feel it is generally risky to be too innovative and adaptive. Planned organizational change happens only periodically—often in response to crisis. This is an especially serious problem because the special services department directors see themselves operating in a more dynamic, changing situation than do directors of any other departments. They report more changes in their responsibilities during the past five years. They also report, however, the smallest amount of departmental contact with groups outside the school system from whom information and help could be obtained. Therefore, they are somewhat isolated and less accepting of demands for change coming from the groups they serve.

Delineation of responsibility at the school level is not clear. Counselors and other personnel assigned to one school are responsible to both the building principal and their respective department head.

All these problems illustrate an earlier point. The basic approach of special services must be changed to make it an effective department. The many strengths the various departments have should enable them to make these changes, but the problems cited above indicate the magnitude of the task.

- With rare exceptions, guidance counselors and advisers work without secretarial assistance so that at least one-third of their time is spent in clerical work.
- Pupil adjustment counselors are paid more than $14,000 a year and yet by contract work from 8:30 to *no later than 2:15*, which rules out visiting homes, working with teachers, or attending in-service meetings in mid- or late afternoon.
- Few recently-trained medical doctors will accept the role of school doctor in Boston. This outdated role does not use the clinic and lab technology conditions of modern medicine.
- School nurses receive annual salaries well above R.N. scales (creating a long waiting list for school jobs), work less than forty weeks, administer few health services, and spend an average of 50 percent of their time on paper work.

- Attendance workers, mostly former policemen and very few with the A.B. degree, are paid more than teachers with M.A. degrees.

The pay scale for these jobs are too high, and the calibre of talent very uneven. Before the school department creates another 100 jobs, it should analyze the work and the levels of skill which will be necessary. Some workers in present jobs will naturally protest any changes that do not upgrade pay and requirements. Pupil personnel experts in other eastern Massachusetts communities can offer useful criticism and suggestions on how to make the special services division more efficient and effective.

Since pupil adjustment counselors must first teach for several years, many qualified candidates with masters' degrees in social work cannot work immediately as adjustment counselors. These social workers would be especially helpful in working with families and social service agencies. A May 1970 study of adjustment counselors for the Boston School Committee urged that the teaching requirement be dropped in favor of other professional and work experience qualifications.

Both adjustment counselors and guidance counselors (the separate "adviser" label for junior high should be dropped and the categories merged) should be considered parallel to teachers in rank and status and paid at the same salary level. Extra pay should be justified only for a longer work year, e.g., an additional two weeks or month to follow through on cases and to check on progress before the fall term begins.

Pupil adjustment counselors should be screened by a team of counselors, psychologists, and social workers. At this time, almost any teacher can qualify for the counselor's position by scoring high on an exam, regardless of his or her qualifications. Veterans go automatically to the top of the list. No one checks on the personal characteristics and clinical skills of the applicants; which may be limited or totally lacking in some instances.

Health services should be reorganized to use fewer nurses and more health aides, to release general practitioner M.D.s and to rely more on neighborhood and community health centers.

Other special services problems include regulations that hinder cooperation and limit the use of computers to store data on individual diagnosis and treatment. Another concern is deciding who should be able to call a work conference of those professionals concerned with an individual child—for example a speech therapist, counselor, and nurse in one case, or an attendance officer, counselor, psychologist, and teacher in another. The need for a team approach to individual and family problems is clear.

Recommendations

- As the Boston School Department has already recognized, special services should be consolidated under a highly qualified individual who would be the associate superintendent for special services.

- The myriad regulations governing each department now in special services should be sharply reduced and updated. The new associate superintendent should form a team of specialists within the system and experts from other agencies which deal with the school system and the special needs of children. Legislative action would be necessary for some changes but many steps could be taken by 1972.

- Teams of special service personnel should be assigned to each district to work under the general direction of the area superintendents so decisions affecting each child might be made at a level close to the student. Each area superintendent should establish an area Health and Pupil Services Council. Ideally, a pupil adjustment counselor should assume major responsibility for convening other specialists. A monitoring mechanism should be created so that a single person cannot subvert any program.

   The school department must guarantee the right to review decisions. Coordination between the Department of Attendance and the Department of Pupil Adjustment Counseling must be developed. Attendance counseling efforts should be therapeutic, not policing actions. Counselors should give special attention in this area to inner city students.

- Specialists in pupil services (for example Adjustment counselors) should be able to enter the system as specialists, not only as former classroom teachers. Panels of outside experts—community people and colleagues—should judge the competence of applicants.

- The ratio of special service personnel to students must eventually be increased. The MACE Report on Pupil Services for Massachusetts Schools recommends the following standards:

School systems should work towards achieving a ratio of one pupil services worker for each 125 students. We suggest as minimal standards the following schedule for achieving the recommended staffing:

$$\begin{array}{ll} \text{in two years} & -1{:}400 \\ \text{in five years} & -1{:}250 \\ \text{in ten years} & -1{:}125 \end{array}$$

Additional counselors and specialists should be hired, as partners to teachers, not as superiors in status and pay. Counselors should serve as members of the instructional teams and as liaison agents with the home and other agencies. No more pupil adjustment counselors should be added nor raises granted until the time limit on a counselor's working day is dropped, and counselors agree to participate in a continuing program of in-service education based on cases and consultations with other professional specialists.

   The new pupil services staff should include child advocates (see section on attendance officers); health aides, who should reduce the reliance on R.N.s (see section on school health); and counselors and psychologists who will work with children and teachers in existing classes and settings.

• The special services ought to be regrouped into two large departments, each headed by an educational leader with high professional qualifications.

A Special Education Department would plan and coordinate instructional programs: programs for the mentally retarded (special classes); programs for students with sensory disorders (new vision-resources, speech and hearing, perceptually handicapped); programs for the emotionally disturbed; and programs for the physically handicapped. These programs should be headed by an assistant director. Several programs might require special supervisors of teachers or therapists.

Many of these programs serve children with multiple handicaps, and many problems require work with the entire family. Staff members must therefore work closely with various counselors and community agencies.

A Pupil Services Department would serve all children and coordinate diagnostic and counseling services: child guidance; pupil adjustment counselors; attendance (officers and child advocates); and health services (medical and mental health). Currently, each of these services has a director (attendance has two co-equal head supervisors), but during the next ten years these services will require a different kind of organization. In the future, most will work out of area offices or in schools.

Guidance Counselors would work in schools as part of the instructional team, with students, parents, teachers, and other specialists.

Social workers (a few of the present adjustment counselors) would work extensively with the students' homes and with community agencies. In cases where legal violations exist, they should be assisted by "child advocates" (community persons) and former police or probation officers. Their work should be coordinated on an area basis.

Nurses for each area would supervise health aides in the schools and coordinate programs of diagnosis and treatment with neighborhood and community health centers. The city of Boston can no longer afford two separate medical and health systems. The difficult transition would require a leader with an ability to design and develop collaborative programs for the City of Boston.

The pupil services coordinator should meet these professional and personal criteria: a doctorate in an area directly related to pupil personnel services; some experience in related work with two or more of the departments he will supervise; an awareness of current developments in all pupil personnel specialties; a demonstrated competence in research and evaluation; participation in developing innovative ideas in the pupil personnel services field; demonstrated administrative ability; and a demonstrated awareness of the need for community support and a willingness to use community resources.

Candidates for this position would be recruited and screened by the associate superintendent for special services with the assistance of outside experts, as recommended in the dean's report.

The coordinator of special education classes should have the same qualifications as the coordinator of pupil services, with emphasis in the special education field.

- The school department should use paraprofessionals in special services, especially in health services and in programs for black and Spanish-speaking families. These aides should be considered semiprofessionals and potential professionals and should be recruited from the various white working class and minority neighborhoods of the city. The school department should establish a career-ladder for their advancement to prepare them ultimately to become full professionals.

- Several problems in the special services area require state action. For example, a student must be evaluated by a psychiatrist to be eligible for the emotionally disturbed program. This is costly ($25 an hour) and subject to delay, given the shortage of psychiatrists. Furthermore, it is difficult to get children evaluated so they may leave these classes or residential schools. The MACE Report on Project 750 (for emotionally disturbed school-age children) recommended that "clinical, counseling, and educational psychologists who are Diplomates of the American Board of Professional Psychology also certify student eligibility." The Boston School Committee should support this recommendation for two reasons: it serves students more efficiently and it costs less.

Boston officials should be aware of two other findings in this MACE report: the first is that an unusually low proportion of black children certified for 750 eligibility are admitted into residential schools reimbursed by the state, and the second that disadvantaged children in general tend to be placed in special classes rather than in residential schools, which some desperately need.

Another problem concerns pupil adjustment counselors. By state standards these counselors must have two or more years of teaching experience. Moreover, their special programs are supervised at the state level by the Division of Youth Services rather than the State Department of Education. Many professionals applaud the emphasis on "prevention" in the pupil adjustment counselor's job. But now the various pupil service workers must function together in the student's interest as a team of collaborators.

Still another problem is one of attitudes—of teachers, administrators, and the general public. The number of special classes keeps growing; yet many experts believe that "re-education" programs, some residential and many involving the whole family are the best solution for emotional problems. Others are at work developing "milieu therapy" that may help a child cope more adequately with himself and his environment. All teachers and administrators must find ways to prevent a child from being excluded or treated in a totally separate site when perhaps counselors, psychologists, and psychiatrists can help the teacher develop strategies to use within the classroom.

These recommendations will create problems with existing staff. Changes could be made in this order: (1) the school department should appoint an associate superintendent in 1970 and two key directors by early 1971, (2) the school department should form one pupil services team per area to test coordination of the pupil adjustment counselor, the attendance officer, the nurse, the counselor, and other specialists who might be needed; (3) each area superintendent should appoint one adjustment counselor in his area to set up and coordinate the pupil services teams.

Meanwhile, the other tasks of revising procedures and transferring medical examinations to various community health centers (as it is now done in Charlestown) could proceed as rapidly as possible. School doctors could in most instances be relieved of the daily obligation to visit each building. They could then assume responsibility for exams in other buildings in the second half of each year until all schools are linked to a city-wide health care plan. By 1975, state and federal grants to these centers should cover the medical, dental, and mental health needs of most of the school population. Psychiatrists currently serve on the staffs of many such centers in Boston and, through the mental health cachement area plan, they could soon serve students.

11 Programs for the Disadvantaged: Title I

School officials can learn a great deal from the Title I experience.

The Background of Title I Planning in Boston

Between 1963 and 1965, when the Elementary and Secondary Education Act (ESEA) was passed, the black community of Boston took issue with the school department over the low amount of money spent to educate their children. In September 1963, the school department established two programs, Operation Counterpoise and Operation Second Chance. Operation Counterpoise which later became the Elementary Enrichment Program, was designed to serve students from disadvantaged backgrounds by providing them with an additional $115 per pupil. Extra teachers and materials were devoted to providing remedial reading and arithmetic. Specialists in art, music and science were hired to teach programs in these areas. In 1965, when Boston received Title I money the program's name was changed to the Elementary Enrichment Program, but it remained the same.

Operation Second Chance, which attempts to keep potential dropouts in school, began as a junior high program. Presently it is in operation in three junior highs. The senior high program has evolved into the work-study program at Boston High School.

Just before Title I arrived in Boston the school system began to develop plans for a "model subsystem." The school department hoped that new teaching techniques and materials could be developed for use in the entire system. The program began in the Boardman Elementary School. Since then, the subsystem has grown to include a junior and senior high school. Later the elementary portion of the program was moved into the new Trotter school, and a preschool program was included.

With Title I funds, the school department began two additional elementary programs—the Individual Progress Program and the Language Transition Program. Under the IPP program, pupils have much individual attention and can progress at their own rate in ungraded classrooms. The Language Transition Program is designed to teach English to non-English-speaking children so that they can successfully cope with regular school instruction.

All these programs are now funded by both Title I funds and local school

125

funds, but because of the way the school budget is kept it is virtually impossible to determine what these programs cost. The cost figures are scattered in at least three different locations: the Title I Department, the various principals' offices, and the system's central business office.

This fragmentation in budgeting is also evident in administration. The general outline of the EEP Program appears in the project proposal the school system submits each year to the State Department of Education for approval. The proposal establishes the general level of *federal* funding for the EEP Program vis-à-vis the other Title I programs. This outline does not concern allocation of resources between school districts or buildings. The associate director of the EEP Program decides allocation of federal resources among districts independent of the proposal. The principals decide allocation of resources among buildings. And within a building, the principal and teachers decide allocation of resources.

For non-Title I funds, the school department's central office staff (the business manager, the associate superintendent of personnel, and the associate superintendent for elementary schools) decides allocation of resources among districts. In a district, the principal decides allocation of non-Title I resources, and for a building the principal and teachers decide.

The decisions concerning how to use money and personnel are also complicated, with no overall control, direction or plan. Although the general goal of the Title I program is stated in the project proposal, the goal is in turn modified by all the subsequent decisions which teachers, supervisors and principals make. It is even difficult to discern what criteria are used by teachers to determine the type of reading program to use. Students rarely are given real diagnostic tests to determine the nature of their reading problems. The standardized test that indicates students are reading below grade level is the only indicator of need. And this test determines neither the cause of the reading deficiency, nor its precise nature.

EEP Planning: The Current Situation and Federal Funds

The first phase of the planning process which concerns *federal* funds involves three parental advisory councils: separate building councils in each Title I school, four area councils with members elected from the building councils, and a city-wide council elected from the four area councils. Simultaneously the EEP director meets with his staff and some parents to discuss the program. The city-wide parental advisory council coordinates and forwards them to the Title I Board, which also receives the plans of the EEP director and his staff. The Title I Board formulates a tentative description of the Title I project for the forthcoming year and sends it to the state Title I office for review.

After he receives comments from the state Title I office, the EEP director begins the second phase of planning: with consultation, he drafts an application and budget for federal funds. He submits this application to the Title I director, who includes it with applications from the other two Title I projects in Boston.

The third phase of the planning process involves obtaining final "sign off" approval from other local community agencies, the state, the board of superintendents, and the school committee. The influential participants in this process are the EEP director and the state and federal governments.

The amount of federal money the program receives is a result of decisions made by the Congress of the United States. If Congress has acted promptly on the education appropriations bill, the amount of money allocated for Title I will be known by July. Recently Congress has delayed enacting appropriations bills, and the precise amount of money available for the fiscal year is unknown until half the fiscal year is over. In this case the Office of Education is permitted to allow a level of Title I spending which does not exceed the level of the previous year. The actual appropriation may be less than the amount available during the previous year, a risk the school system takes when it goes ahead with the Title I operations in the fall.

Evaluation: An Overview of the Present Situation

Four kinds of evaluation are supposedly built into the planning cycle: fiscal evaluation, research into the needs of the pupils, end-of-the-year evaluation, and process evaluation. Fiscal evaluation is the accounting for money spent on the program during the year. There are three important purposes to this effort. This evaluation establishes that money has not been spent for purposes that Title I regulations do not permit. It establishes that consultants and teachers have participated in the Title I program before they are paid. And it insures that the program adheres to the budget.

Assessment of student needs is based on the standardized achievement tests that are given twice a year. In the end-of-year evaluation, little effort seems to have been made to relate a student's gains from the previous year's program to what he will need in the coming year.

The school system has made no attempts to determine how well a particular program has succeeded for EEP pupils, and thus officials cannot make decisions about program modification. End-of-the-year evaluation is needed to consider the program's overall effects on the target population.

In the EEP program, three assistant directors oversee process evaluation—the constant monitoring of the program—to see it is carried out according to plan and to make sure unexpected problems are solved. However, often there is not a specific program to monitor. Thus these assistant directors check only that general program guides are followed.

Evaluation has had no impact on program planning or modification. The Model Demonstration Subsystem has never been evaluated, except that end-of-the-year test scores are reported, without analysis, to the state. The work-study program was evaluated only once. But because the report was not completely favorable, it was shelved. Evaluation of the EEP program is done only because federal regulations require them to remain eligible for funds.

Evaluation: The Current Problem

Many problems limit the EEP evaluation program. First, the program's objectives are too broad. EEP's stated objectives are: to improve classroom performance in reading beyond usual expectations; to improve performance in mathematics for those children who have serious deficiencies in this area; to encourage positive pupil attitudes toward education; and to discover and develop latent talents of pupils.

What are the "usual expectations" for reading performance? Are the same expectations realistic for all pupils? Is there a difference between "classroom performance" and reading performance on standardized tests? If so, why are standardized tests used to measure "classroom performance?"

Which children are considered to have a "serious deficiency" in mathematics? And how does an official determine whether pupils have a "positive attitude toward education?" Does "education" mean "school?" Finally, one must define "latent talents" before one can discover and develop them.

Many program administrators do not want systematic, external evaluations from independent observers. For this reason, cooperation between program planners and evaluators tends to break down. Program goals are not clearly defined for evaluation, and evaluators tend to produce reports that decision-makers cannot use to make program modifications.

Evaluation efforts tend to concentrate on a few types of academic achievement, with little attention to behavioral and attitudinal dimensions of the program (e.g., student self-concept, motivation) and no attention to uncovering the program's unexpected results. Also, obtaining evaluation results often takes too long.

The school department should coordinate the Title I evaluation office and the Department of Educational Investigation and Measurement. Presently, the Department of Educational Investigation and Measurement, which conducts the city-wide standardized testing program, can and does change tests from year to year, and even from the fall to the spring of the school year. These changes damage the Title I evaluation program because it makes impossible comparisons between years and between the beginning and the end of the year.

Too often, the reports do not specifically evaluate the program's results in terms of its original objectives. Also, the reports are usually noncumulative. To date, the school system cannot judge the cumulative impact of the EEP program.

Finally, past reports provide no information about cost versus effectiveness of the existing program compared to other compensatory programs in the area or in the nation.

A Planning and Evaluation Model

First, the system should move towards an appropriate Planning, Programing, Budgeting, Evaluation System (PPBES). With the present system, it is virtually impossible for the planners in the school system to determine precisely what the Title I program costs.

Second, the program's objectives should be stated more specifically. Unless the school department can evaluate specific aspects of the program, it cannot modify either its goals or its relevancy to the changing environment.

Third, a variety of people should participate in the planning process. Teachers, consultants, independent professional evaluators, administrators, parents, and students could provide varied contributions.

Fourth, planning must begin with an accurate assessment of needs. To make this assessment, the Title I staff should use not only standardized tests, but also less conventional methods—which expert consultants could suggest.

Fifth, the Title I staff should work with clearly-defined guidelines. Such guidelines would foster financial and intellectual coordination and increase possibilities for effective program evaluation and modification.

Sixth, the Title I staff should work out program plans in greater detail than they now do. The program should have specific goals and subgoals.

Seventh, Title I funds should be concentrated so that in-service training, more detailed planning efforts, and truly individualized instruction can become possible. Allocating $150 per student is unlikely to produce significant gains in performance. Increasing the funding level to $250 per student, however, makes it feasible to experiment with new, more costly techniques. The Title I staff should also seek additional city and state funds to provide additional services and programs in other sections of the city with low income families who could benefit from IPP, EEP, or field trips.

Eighth, if people operating within the program guidelines are given discretion to make program decisions, they must coordinate and record these decisions.

Ninth, planners should consider alternatives to the Title I program which cost approximately the same. Planners should be critical of the existing program and open to new methods.

Recommendations

- The school department should support the Educational Research Corporation's proposal for an information system and data bank on elementary students. This system would supply information for use in program evaluation.

- The Boston School Department should hire (at least as a consultant) a full-time person with professional experience in research and program evaluation. This expert could work with Title I planners to develop the program and help them define objectives that will naturally lead to evaluation.
- The Title I staff should evaluate all programs. If conventional standardized tests cannot accurately measure the success of a program (such as the Model Demonstration Subsystem), the staff must develop suitable measurement techniques and evaluation designs. Without adequate evaluation, experimental programs will never be introduced throughout the school system.
- Evaluation techniques should not be limited to the use of standardized tests. The Title staff should use other measures for evaluation, including in-depth interviews with students, analysis of writing samples, recorded reading sessions, carefully designed questionnaires, actual classroom observation using a uniform observation instrument, and tests of creative and critical thinking.
- The Title I staff should develop evaluation techniques which will yield useful information for decision-makers. Techniques should also be developed to yield information for program modification.
- Official, formal, organization arrangements should be made to assure that planners and evaluators cooperate with each other and that program administrators or operators do not sabotage the work of evaluators. The Department of Educational Measurement and the computer center should be used by evaluation personnel. The evaluator should have immediate and direct access to the computer center, which should have standing orders to comply with all evaluation requests. The evaluator should not need to be cleared by an associate superintendent to use computer hardware or software. The Department of Educational Measurement and Investigation (or its successor) should not be permitted to change tests or institute new tests without approval of the program evaluator.
- The Title I staff and planning staff should develop an overall evaluation plan.
- The Title I staff should distribute widely its evaluation reports to staff and to citizens. Sufficient copies of each evaluation report should be printed to assure school staff, parents, and the public easy access to it.
- Boston should try to establish cooperative evaluation efforts with other school systems. Such cooperation would permit interprogram comparisons, cost savings and program improvement.
- The school department should make program evaluations based on specific performance criteria related to objectives set at the beginning of a project. The department should also assess whether the project results should be compared to other projects with similar goals.

12 Management Services

Measurement, Research and Evaluation

The Department of Educational Investigation and Measurement, established in 1914, has evolved into a strong but fiercely independent arm of the system. The department has resisted using computers to speed test correction and dissemination and sharing the findings with others.

Yet, teachers in the Title I program must evaluate their success. School officials, recognizing the inherent conflict, propose a new Department of Research and Evaluation which would combine the functions of Title I evaluation with those of the Investigation and Measurement staff. A new director would be selected from within the system.

In the long run, the new department should probably be closely linked to educational and budgetary planning. But the most urgent immediate need is close cooperation with special education and pupil services. The department would also need to plan more rigorous Title I evaluations and then expand the evaluation function to include all state and local programs and to provide an "accountability profile" for each school.

The department would have two separate but related functions: (1) diagnosing and evaluating individual student needs, using individualized tests (Stanford-Binet, Rorschak, etc.), and consulting with various counselors, parents, and other educators about placing students in special or regular classes (and in some cases including the students return to classes); and (2) planning, administrating and analyzing group tests of ability, achievement, or attitudes for the city as a whole and for areas and schools as they indicate a need for program evaluation.

The department, with assistance from the educational data-processing center, should be able to provide teachers with profiles of their classes' performance (as is the case in many Title I classrooms now); to provide students and parents with data on student skills; and to provide local school officials and councils information about schools' strengths and needs. These data should be used to question past performance, to plan more carefully revised programs and to justify requests for additional or different staff and materials.

Principals and area staff would need more training in measurement and evaluation to assess the extent of their needs. A more substantial data-processing staff and budget would also be necessary, for special printouts would be needed whenever a sub-test or certain test items reveal a pattern of problems.

In some cases, the testing program does not distinguish between the retarded student and a student whose verbal problem results from his recent arrival in Boston—whether the student is from Puerto Rico, Florida, or West Virginia. Recently, parents have sued the school system on this issue.

The Director and assistant directors of this department would need advanced technical training. Salaries of $20,000 and above are sufficient to attract the best doctorates in the evaluation of instruction who have valuable urban education experience. Four or five courses in testing and measurement taken on a part-time basis would not provide sufficient competence.

Department of Public Information

During the 1960s the Boston School Department was severely criticized in newspapers, at hearings of state and federal agencies such as the U.S. Civil Rights Commission, and in books which described Boston schools. A new breed of education reporters and critics began to focus on urban education.

For many years the Boston School Department relied on an office of publicity and statistics to compile information which the press needed. However, this office's major activity was to publish the annual statistical reports which the Commonwealth required. In the late 1960s, a new department was formed to provide information to the public directly and through the mass media.

Currently a director and a consultant prepare weekly news releases, plan a weekly radio show, brief media representatives, produce a staff newsletter to inform school system employees of recent department developments, and publish the Boston School Department annual report.

Television and radio staff members, none of whom specializes in education, rely heavily on school officials for presentation of their side of a question, especially on high conflict issues. Education reporters for the newspapers who specialize on school matters research stories for themselves rather than rely on prepared releases. An increase in public information staff or news releases would probably increase friction between the school department and education reporters.

The system newsletter and modern annual report inform people within the system of recent developments and appointments. In recent annual reports the department has concentrated on new curricula, cooperative university relationships, and attempts to develop new approaches.

Some top officials believe that an expanded public information and community relations staff might further reduce the gap between criticism and system responsiveness. However, many community spokesmen emphasize the school committee's temptation to rely on a public relations staff to improve their image and to gloss over genuine problems. They wonder whether such a staff can be kept out of political campaigns for various offices.

A major urban school system needs a small staff to present its needs and accomplishments to the public. Community relations, however, can be best handled at the school and area level, not from a central office. Teachers, counselors, and administrators must perform satisfactorily or a school system will never recapture a formable "image."

Maintenance, Alterations, and Repair

Both teachers and parents of Boston school children complain about broken windows, insufficient heat, and unrepaired fixtures in Boston schools. School officials also complain about the facilities for central school headquarters on Beacon and Myrtle Streets.

A statue, unique to Boston, specifies a certain amount for school alterations and repairs each year. In 1970, school officials won a substantial change in the formula. In the past, employee groups and school committees have frequently agreed to allocate less money for school repairs so that more money could be spent on staff salaries.

Also, the school department has sought emergency loans for extraordinary repairs. Several administrations have agreed to borrow money to try to improve school buildings in Boston. Currently money is needed to renovate and upgrade senior high facilities which expert accreditation teams find inadequate.

Many teachers and principals are concerned about the process for securing action on necessary school repairs. Requisitions compete with one another for attention, and principals are usually blamed for the inaction. Given the scarcity of resources, priority often goes to the parent or community groups most willing to march on Beacon Street or flood the switchboard with angry calls.

Budgeting and planning is a second problem. Only the Director of Planning and Engineering and his staff appear to know what priorities are. The annual budget discussions do not include specific lists of projects, problems, and priorities. The 1970 Alterations and Repair Budget simply specified total amounts, not how much was allocated for each school, nor how much for emergencies. It did not have a breakdown by buildings or grounds, fire protection or furniture.

Salaries	$ 720,000
Workmen's compensation	1,000
Pensions	70,000
Administration expenses other than salaries	59,000
General alterations and repairs	6,378,161
Total	$7,228,661

Also, there are inequities among schools. The oldest and most famous schools—Latin and English—have special endowment funds and other sources headmasters may tap for necessary alterations and renovations. The newer high schools and district schools have no such sources. Federal funds can be used to an extent to prepare a facility for a new program. But some facilities badly need repairs for more basic reasons—such as children's safety and health, especially in winter.

The current staff of more than fifty planning, engineering and repair specialists is centralized. The Director of Planning and Engineering, formerly the Chief Structural Engineer, traditionally reports to the superintendent of schools. In practice, he appears frequently before the school committee, and responds to their concerns by reporting on completed or future action. His presentations are always detailed and delivered with an enthusiasm and optimism that should characterize public officials at all levels of government.

The Boston Finance Commission has recently studied the way in which minor repairs are contracted out to firms, a practice which the 1944 Strayer Report indicated should cease. They concluded that the volume of service order work described as "emergency in nature" was disturbingly high, and that much of the furniture and lock repair work could be done by a small repair staff—another Strayer recommendation not adopted, although by 1972 custodians were issued tools for just this purpose.

The Finance Commission recommendations of July 2, 1970, are summarized to insure their wider circulation. They could contribute to greater efficiency and economy.

Recommendations

- A small repair staff should be recruited to undertake routine repair work now performed by private contractors.
- The school committee should consider using custodial staff to handle certain repairs of a routine and minor character.
- Although the number of contractors used in school repair work increased from 1968 to 1969, the Department of Planning and Engineering should further expand its circle of available contractors by using the additional list of 106 firms compiled by the Finance Commission, which will be sent to the Department of Planning and Engineering.
- The designation "emergency" as applied to school building repair work should be strictly defined to mean only those cases in which a threat to health, safety, or continuation of schoolroom operation is involved.
- The bulk of repair work should be set up on a district basis for unit price bidding by contractors. Glass replacement is already set up satisfactorily on such a basis. Unit price, as understood, means a bid by a contractor for a basic unit of labor and materials for any of the categories of repair.

The second recommendation suggesting the use of custodians for repairs fails to recognize the realities of labor negotiations. The custodial contract would have to be changed to designate a new category such as "junior custodian-repair man" (or "mechanic" or "handyman"). This category should be negotiated at a rate between the current junior and senior designations, and should attract the more skillful and ambitious young custodians who could be quickly trained in furniture, lock, window, and related repair work. The school department could develop incentive and bonus programs for maintenance and operation crews which, by preventative action, reduce the number of repairs.

Recommendations

- The department should be renamed the Department of School Maintenance. The planning functions should be shifted to the planning center and to an associate superintendent for planning, allowing for specialization in maintaining schools already built.
- The director and the business manager should assume responsibility for developing a detailed budget, school by school and project by project (at least those above $1000). The director should report to the business manager and submit weekly and monthly progress reports and plans.
- The department should recruit a small repair crew to be assigned to tasks by the area superintendent and the director.
- In each secondary school or elementary school district, one junior custodian should be designated "custodian-repair man" at a salary high enough to make the assignment attractive and competitive.
- As the department revises a program budget, the separate budget for Alterations and Repairs should be abolished, and projects should be considered with other priorities in a single school department budget.

13 The Schools and the Resources of the City

This chapter deals with the sharing of resources among Boston's schools and its cultural resources, universities, and businesses.

Cultural Resources and the Schools

The fine arts in Boston have traditionally been a privately supported elitist preserve.[a] The separation of art and practical life have probably been more "fastidiously cultivated" in Boston than in other American cities. However, this classic separation is economically unsound, for the elite alone can no longer support the aesthetic domain. Social and economic realities suggest collaborative programs between the public schools and cultural organizations.

How can the educational and cultural communities work together? Resources and money for promoting these collaborative programs are limited, but imaginative use of untapped resources could result in improvements in existing programs as well as development of new ones.

Boston holds many institutions and organizations dedicated to artistic and intellectual endeavors. The city has a privately supported Museum of Fine Arts, Opera Company, Ballet, and Symphony Orchestra, as well as many smaller performing arts companies—primarily in music and the theater. Over twenty companies are involved in performing arts in Boston. Greater Boston sponsors ten performing arts groups and thirty-two museums. Neighborhood centers offer fine and performing arts, as do commercial galleries and practicing artists living in the area.

Universities and colleges, historical display areas (there are over 100 in Greater Boston), and institutions which focus on science and nature—the Museum of Science, the New England Aquarium, the Franklin Park Zoo and the Audubon preserves, particularly Drumlin Farm in nearby Lincoln—are also traditional cultural resources. Not surprisingly, most large-scale collaborative programs between the schools and the cultural community have developed with major museums and performing arts groups of the city. The schools use smaller museums, display areas, and fine and performing arts groups less frequently.

Yet these groups do not fully describe Boston's rich, diverse culture. Boston, in its roles of major city, seaport, regional commerce and transportation center, state capitol, and historic immigration site, houses groups and institutions that

[a]Bernard Taper, THE ARTS IN BOSTON, Harvard University Press, Cambridge, 1970.

137

represent modern urban industrial civilization and its component ethnic sub-groups.

Additional cultural resources in Boston would include government agencies (e.g., the Federal Food and Drug Commission), the court system, the Boston Public Library, nonprofit service organizations from the Red Cross to the Junior League, professional groups (including businesses concerned with educational problems in general and Boston public schools in particular), the mass media—newspapers, radio, and television—and ethnic groups of the city.

The school department should examine the content and general format of programs that exist between the schools and cultural institutions. The largest cooperative programs are the yearly field trips for elementary and junior high school children. These trips are organized on a system-wide basis and follow a standard format. They usually are one-time only visits to historical display areas, museums, or nature preserves. They require buses for transportation, involve large group tours or lecture-demonstration, and have limited orientation or follow-up. An exception to this pattern is the program the school department developed with the Museum of Fine Arts in 1969-1970. The museum, with the School Volunteers of Boston and administrators of the school system, planned a series of orientation lectures given by museum-trained volunteers. These volunteers visited classrooms before the students visited the Museum, showed slides and answered questions. The program was so successful that it was a model for other field trip orientation programs during 1970-1971. These field trips include more than half the total student population every year, and they represent a major expenditure in collaborative programs.

Slight variations in the general format come from special programs like the Boston Children's Opera, sponsored in 1970 by the Junior League; the Boston Symphony Orchestra concerts; and the Young Audiences concerts. These are also coordinated through the central school office, but they involve fewer students (6 percent each year, approximately 5,000 in 1969) and offer opportunities for small group discussion and orientation and follow-up work in the classrooms.

The schools also select a limited number of students or teachers in fine arts or science classes to participate in workshops. These are sometimes organized through central office personnel, or the community institutions offer them to the schools on a first-come, first-served basis.

Some school programs are initiated by individual schools or classes, sometimes with aid from the School Volunteers of Boston. These programs include field trips to some of the less visited display areas, businesses, government agencies, and nonprofit service organizations. Sometimes they include guest speakers and the use of materials provided by outside groups.

The school department should examine the features of major programs. Does a centrally scheduled trip on a bus increase a student's independence and mobility, or does it merely provide a minimal interruption in school routine?

Does a short visit with a large group lecture-demonstration increase a student's appreciation of a cultural institution's unique offerings, motivating him to return at a later date? Does it develop his perceptual skills and increase his social or aesthetic understanding? Does it add to curriculum content in a way lectures in the classroom cannot?

The present programs are inadequate. There is no in-depth exposure to any of the institutions and organizations which make up Boston's cultural community. Isolated visits tend to be unsuccessful in building understanding, appreciation, and skills. Programs designed to be more valuable—the Boston Museum of Fine Arts parents' pass program, the EDCO (Educational Collaborative) fine arts workshops and Arts 6 experience in Brookline have not been as successful as their planners hoped.

The programs should not be discontinued. Instead, school officials must clarify the goals of the programs and use available resources in more innovative ways. Some changes in format and administration of collaborative programs would result in expansion and improvement at minimal cost.

First, the format could be rearranged. For example, many students could benefit from listening to records in the classroom, making their own musical instruments, and having a musician visit once or several times. Transporting them to a Boston Symphony Orchestra concert would not necessarily be a better experience. The cost of the in-class program might be the same or less.

Symphony concerts for many students might be more suitable at the secondary school level as the culmination of a carefully planned music curriculum which had extended throughout the lower grades. Some students should attend at least three or four times as part of the possible exploration of a career in music or just because they take special delight in music. One resource, therefore, is not better or worse than another. Each has its unique qualities which teachers should recognize and match carefully with a student's particular needs.

Perhaps the school department could develop a curriculum centered around the city itself. Teachers could take younger children on walking tours of their immediate neighborhoods and gradually expand the geographical scope of these programs, using public transportation whenever possible to increase the students' awareness of various ways to move about the city. This curriculum might be organized around various aspects of city life: economic, political, social, ecological, recreational, aesthetic, and educational. It could include taking trips outside the school and inviting visitors into the school. High school students would know the city well enough to undertake independent study projects as part of their regular course work or to participate in apprenticeship programs spending a few hours work each week working with local theater groups, museum curators, landscape architects, government agencies, or local radio and television stations.

These programs should include educating parents and citizens about the goals of collaboration, rescheduling school time, and reorganizing credit requirements in the schools.

These programs would also involve changing certain administrative practices in the schools. At this time the two major sources of initiative for collaborative efforts are personnel from individual schools and from outside groups—members of organizations like the School Volunteers of Boston, the Junior League, and EDCO, or staff from institutions and groups, like the Audubon Society, the Children's Museum, or the Museum of Fine Arts. In these programs, the school system's central office personnel act mainly as coordinators—scheduling buses, visits, interviews. However, the collaborative programs have no centralized information mechanism and the programs rarely expand. Those areas that are not represented by special Boston school departments—drama, dance, and school libraries—do not expand at all. The lack of communication and coordination is a crucial factor at the local school level, for teachers simply do not know about available community resources.

Fewer problems arise from those programs which members of the cultural community or other outside groups originate and coordinate. These programs generally limit the number of students involved. They would undoubtedly increase if the school system would coordinate efforts and information about them.

The general lack of overall planning, coordination, communication, and evaluation among the various departments involved with community cultural programs is undoubtedly hindering effective development of good collaborative efforts. The school system clearly has great needs and few resources to match the services community groups and institutions offer. And the available resources are not presently being used fully. The school system must work with community organizations in flexible, efficient ways. Changes at the system level, in the individual school, and in the resources themselves seem necessary to develop more extensive programs of high quality.

Recommendations for System-Level Changes

- A community resources coordinator in the curriculum office should coordinate programs involving businesses, cultural organizations, health and medical facilities, and other groups outside the school system.
- A council composed of members of the Boston artistic and cultural community (e.g., M.E.C.A.), parents, area superintendents, and a central office representative should meet regularly to facilitate communication among groups in the cultural community and the school system. This group would be established to collect and disseminate information and to advise in establishing new programs.
- The area superintendents' offices should plan, implement, and evaluate

programs. They should also cooperatively determine individual district needs and resources. And they should convey information to the central office staff.

- The Boston schools, through EDCO, should develop a metropolitan artistic and cultural program, which could set guidelines for use of resources and coordinate ties with neighborhood centers, Summerthing, the Mayor's Office of Cultural Affairs, and the Bicentennial Office. A more extensive definition and identification of Boston's cultural resources would provide valuable untapped materials and personnel for educational programs.
- The School Volunteers should continue to organize programs, and if possible they should expand their operations. School officials could use their help to establish programs similar to the one at the Museum of Fine Arts.
- Each school should have a local activities fund to support trips and use of outside materials and speakers. Schools must now depend on money they raise in picture sales and lost book fines or, in some cases, as contributions from local Home and School Associations. This obviously results in an unequal, inadequate, and uncertain distribution of funds available for planning activities. The school department should make direct allocations to each principal to supplement these sources of funds. Each school should also try to locate inexpensive or free resources and to make this information available to the central office.
- Other funds might come from expanded financing of state and federal programs in the arts and humanities.
- Teacher workshops and programs of in-service training could develop skills and curriculum necessary for teachers' maximum use of outside resources. The school department should encourage schools to use paraprofessional personnel and volunteers in these areas. They should also encourage schools to develop programs that integrate the creative arts and other cultural areas into the basic curriculum.

Recommended Changes within
Individual Schools

- The school department should help establish clear channels for the flow of information about available cultural programs. It should also circulate a cultural and community resources directory for teachers.
- Junior and senior high schools should develop programs in which aides and volunteers will cover classes so all classes may take advantage of outside resources. Flexible scheduling could provide time in which teachers could meet with individual classes and plan special activities—projects, trips, or speakers.
- School officials should encourage a more flexible attitude about course credit

requirements and about work that can receive credit in an individual course. Although some teachers encourage individual students' initiative, the school department must acknowledge and encourage individual research projects outside the classrooms.

Cultural Resources for Urban Education

- Personnel in museums and other cultural organizations are concerned that their present extra curricular programs are not reaching many city children. The school department could help them by better identifying their urban clients and by more effectively promoting existing services in city schools.
- The school department should help develop new formulas and techniques that would appeal to Boston students in system-wide programs. Possibilities might include a mobile art van which could be sent to schools to stimulate workshops in fine and performing arts; loan programs of inexpensive reproductions of art works for classroom use; or store front or school museums.
- Adequate funding for these programs is crucial. In THE ARTS IN BOSTON, Bernard Taper stated that three-fourths of the twenty major Boston organizations devoted to the arts reported budget deficits in 1968. It is difficult to request help from organizations struggling for their own existences. Until assistance comes from governmental or other sources, these organizations should try to develop extensive volunteer programs, like the one at the Museum of Fine Arts. High School students should be included in these volunteer or apprenticeship programs and should receive academic credit for their participation. Smaller organizations might not be able to sustain large-scale activities, but they can make valuable contributions to individual students or small groups.

Business Resources of Boston

During the 1950s and early 1960s, with isolated exceptions, the Boston business[b] community turned its back on the Boston schools. Business leaders regarded the system as too political and unwilling to change. They supported urban critics, programs and laws which penalized the schools. The climate may now be changing as members of the school committee and staff welcome business assistance and support mutual ventures of which Boston High School is a good example.

Industry's expanding awareness of social problems, triggered partly by the

---

[b]"Business" and "Industry" will be used interchangeably in this section, and are defined as the private, profit-motivated sector of our economy.

nation's war on poverty, has led many businessmen to conclude that our cities need good schools to survive. Much of industry's past involvement in schools has been motivated primarily by the need for trained manpower for plants and offices. However, the range of volunteer services the private sector of our economy provides to the public schools has broadened in recent years.

Two recent surveys of businesses' attitudes toward urban social problems indicate that industry is interested in becoming actively involved to improve education. In 1968, the National Industrial Conference Board conducted a study of volunteer participation in public affairs of over 1,000 companies. Five of the fourteen problem areas identified by the study were associated with education and training. Close to half of the companies studied indicated strong interest in participating in improving these areas.

In September 1969, FORTUNE magazine surveyed 500 corporations to determine how business might help solve a number of social problems. The survey revealed that business was becoming involved in social issues in ways which extended far beyond their traditional quest for profits. Most business representatives felt that "supporting education" should be given highest priority. During the last five years, research has identified over fifty specific types of not-for-profit activities and services provided by industry to public schools:

- Improving instructional programs in classrooms, shops and science laboratories
- Participating in cooperative education and work/study programs
- Providing job placement and career guidance information and services
- Assisting teachers in professional growth programs
- Providing student recognition incentive programs
- Participating in curriculum revision, expansion, and evaluation activities
- Providing administrative and staff support services
- Participating in public relations activities of the schools
- Providing material and financial resources

Although the case for collaboration is persuasive, until the late 1960s most relationships in the nation were limited to the traditional vocational education-business education advisory councils. However, the last five years have revealed more extensive industry-education collaborations. The result has been that proponents of the cooperative education model can now point to several concrete instances of collaboration. A recent study, for example, identified educational partnerships between thirty-three companies and thirty-two schools in twenty-three cities. The companies and schools had developed seventy-six specific projects, including curriculum revision, teacher training, administrative assistance, equipment donation, and loaned personnel to work with students in a variety of capacities.

In Boston, a number of industry-education cooperative efforts exist now on which additional relationships can be built. Boston High School has succeeded in utilizing the resources of nearly seventy companies to keep potential dropouts in school and in jobs. Although they meet infrequently, advisory councils for vocational education, business education, and distributive education are available to assist the schools. The School Volunteer Project provides classroom help, primarily school aides, to schools. The New England Telephone Company has financed a study designed to upgrade the activities of the school department's audio-visual department.

These relationships have barely scratched the surface of what might be a tremendous resource for helping the school system. Several companies have indicated interest in working more closely with programs and schools in which mutual interest in collaboration exists. Among these:

- New England Mutual Life Insurance Company has joined forces with central office staff to study the possibility of forming an industry-education council.
- Representatives from the Associated Industries of Massachusetts and the Department of Vocation-Technical Education have planned to meet to examine vocational programs and community needs.
- New England Merchant's Bank has offered to assist the curriculum department.
- Polaroid representatives have met with the director of community relations to examine ways to facilitate better school-community relations.
- New England Mutual has offered its services to enhance a better public image of the school system.
- New England Telephone Company worked with the faculty of Dorchester High School.

The foundation has been established on which to develop new industry-education relationships in Boston. Although the initiative to create collaborative associations rests with the school department, the mayor's office and the business community must demonstrate their continued interest in supporting collaboration.

The mayor's office can provide leadership to demonstrate the importance of close relationships among schools, businesses, cultural centers, government organizations, day-care centers and health-medical facilities. Clearly, city hall initiative, imagination, and support are crucial to foster collaborative efforts among these groups.

Developing skilled manpower depends on an effective educational program which can be significantly expanded and improved through closer association with the business community. Business expertise in management, resource allocation and administrative training can be valuable to educators committed to improving the administration of the Boston School Department. Although previous efforts by business to cooperate with the schools may not have fulfilled their expectations, the industrial community must renew its commitment to assist where help is needed and requested. The Chamber of Commerce and the Associated Industries of Massachusetts must provide leadership. These two groups cannot and must not continue to believe that Boston business can thrive without a close substantial interest in the city's schools.

Some Guidelines for Establishing
Industry-Education Relationships

The school department must consider several basic rules to establish an effective relationship with the Boston business community as it makes further efforts to involve business in public education. They include:

Initiative. For collaboration to succeed, educators must evaluate their program needs to identify those to which business might be responsive. Experience has demonstrated that when businessmen are asked "How can you help us?", they find it difficult to respond. But when educators specifically identify their needs, business can and will respond more positively. Educators must contact businesses, outline proposals, and then wait for business reaction.

Mutual Benefit. Although altruism may be sufficient justification for an initial involvement in education, business frequently must have a clear description of the potential for profit before it will agree to substantive associations. On the other hand, several major Boston firms have as a larger interest the survival of Boston as a major center of civilization and culture. They recognize that schools are vital to this survival.

Corporate Approval. After business-education projects are established, top management will have to approve program alteration or expansion into new forms of collaboration. Educators should recognize that corporate support is essential for sustaining and expanding any industry-education relationship, even though cooperation at lower levels may determine the fulfillment of program goals. At higher levels, the superintendent's and school committee's support of these projects is essential to their success.

Communications. The school department should establish a formal system for communicating with business to encourage the exchange of proposals, opinions, criticisms, and evaluations of the relationships. Although much of the contact between school personnel and business representatives will be informal, other urban school systems have needed an open forum in which to exchange ideas.

Program Size. Although the goal may be to establish an extensive relationship with business, school officials will find industry more receptive to an effort that involves a small initial commitment. From that initial association, representatives can build further relationships based on their favorable experiences. Success breeds the confidence which could ultimately lead to increased business interest in helping schools meet their needs and solve their problems. This has happened with the Boston High School program, which has expanded because its initial success fostered mutual confidence.

The Profit Motive. School officials must recognize that business is profit-oriented, that its resources are not unlimited, and that its interest in assisting schools will fluctuate with economic growth. Many groups compete for corporation grants. Companies are often more willing and able to share staff, space, and equipment with schools than to provide cash grants. Although industry may truly favor school-business collaboration, the realities of profit-loss statements will dictate the extent of that collaboration.

Labor Involvement. Labor unions must also be involved in collaboration efforts, particularly in work-study programs. Boston schools officials are properly sensitive to the concerns of organized labor. Unions are as powerful as management in developing apprenticeship opportunities in trades and industry for members of minority groups. School officials can avoid conflict between unions and industry by involving union representatives in school-business cooperative programs in which union interests may be affected.

Recommendations

First, the school committee must reestablish an industry/education council in Boston. It should meet regularly and frequently to coordinate school needs and business resources and would act as a clearinghouse for information about new approaches for cooperation. One of its first tasks should be creating a "Business Resources Directory" to identify areas in which the business community is interested in assisting schools. Its membership should include principals, area superintendents, school department central office staff, and business leaders (at the vice president-director level). Members of the Chamber of Commerce, the Associated Industries of Massachusetts, and the Central Labor Council should have an integral role in this council.

Second, a member of the school department planning staff should assume major responsibility for organizing collaborative school-business relationships. This official should have ultimate responsibility for equitable distribution of business assistance throughout the school system. He should work closely with the area superintendents, making business resources available to them as they request or need them.

Each area superintendent should be a member of the Industry/Education

Council, and should work with the community resources coordinator to locate available business resources in each area and to allocate these resources to all districts in the city.

Third, the Report of the Massachusetts Task Force for School Business Management offers some valuable recommendations to improve the noninstructional operation of the Commonwealth's schools. Nearly one-half of the businessmen participating in this study represent Boston-based businesses, and the school department could call upon them for further help in improving the local school system. The community resources coordinator should establish contact with each of these businesses as soon as possible.

Fourth, the superintendent should examine the potential for additional forms of industry/education collaboration. Collaboration could result in a downtown high school using resources which business, cultural, health/medical, and government facilities can provide. The varied resources of the urban community environment can provide an alternative form of education for those who desire it.

The school department could explore the potential for contractual arrangements with interested businesses (e.g., education industries or publishing houses) to teach reading and/or math to disadvantaged youth. Educators are developing similar programs elsewhere (Texarkana, San Diego) using financial support from the U.S. Office of Education. Early results indicate that achievement levels may be raised significantly. Performance contracts like these could enable the school department to sponsor experimental approaches for educating underachievers and potential dropouts.[c]

Tripartite association among the business community, local graduate schools of management, and the school department could provide special in-service administrative training programs for principals, vice principals, and department heads. Not only can management techniques be useful in developing better efficiencies in education, but they can contribute to an environment of creativity, self-improvement, improved goal-setting, and team efforts.

University Resources

Boston's unique relationship to higher education has become increasingly important in recent years. Problems of American cities have captured the attention of university students, faculties, and administrations. Many universities are seeking to redefine their roles in recognizing and solving critical social issues of the day. Much of this interest has focused on the problems of the cities and in particular on the new challenges facing urban educational systems.

In Boston, as in other cities, the universities can use the local urban

---

[c]In July 1970 the school committee voted approval of a performance contract concerning the improvement of reading at the Dearborn School with Title I, ESEA funds.

educational system as an important training ground for teachers, counselors, and administrators. And for the Boston schools, the metropolitan universities provide a useful source of information and expertise on current educational problems.

The Boston School-University Relationship

The history of the Boston school-university relationship includes few cooperative ventures before 1960. In the early 1960s the school department officially added "university relations" to the responsibilities of the associate superintendent for curriculum development and educational planning (the current title). Infusion of federal funds through the Elementary and Secondary Education Act of 1965 stimulated an increase in the number of school-university contacts. Projects ranged from involvement by individuals to involvement between large units of universities (usually from the schools of education or medical schools) and a single school or department of the school system.

These common projects were generally successful; however, failures and misunderstandings sometimes developed as obstacles to continued collaboration. Between November 1968 and July 1969, the Danforth Foundation Study of Large City School Systems gathered data through questionnaires and interviews with university personnel who had worked with the Boston public schools and administrators in the school system.

Interviews indicated that both the universities and the schools held views which were preventing more efficient productive relationships. From the university viewpoint, the school department was too bureaucratic and rigid; it was not open to university research needs. Some universities felt that the school system was too defensive and that schools had frequently taken advantage of the universities' interest for their own ends. School personnel, on the other hand, saw universities as ivory towers, with no permanent commitment to the city's problems. School officials felt that universities had not always observed confidentiality and that they had fostered dependency relationships.

These findings were presented to both school and university representatives during a one-day workshop on January 28, 1970. During the workshop, Boston school participants sought to identify the types of relationship and the areas in which they wished to collaborate with the universities. Prominent among Boston School Department objectives were the training of teachers and administrators for work in city schools, and assistance in evaluating school programs and curriculum development.

An afternoon session focused on the obstacles to cooperation which stem from the contrasting organizational structures of the school system and the universities. The decentralized structure and relative independence of the different units in the university organization make it impossible to identify an individual or single office with final authority to commit university's resources to outside projects. Organizations which want university cooperation are often not sure with whom they must deal or what procedures they should follow. Often, a school official's success at receiving university help depends on the interest or enthusiasm of a university specialist.

An awareness of substantial blocks to cooperation *among* universities in the Boston area also emerged during the workshop. The history of poor cooperation among universities made it unlikely that the universities represented would be able to agree on a common set of priorities which they might match against the school department's objectives. The workshop participants concluded that recommendations for improved school-university relations would have to consider both the decentralized structure of the universities and the unlikelihood that collectively universities would be able to agree upon a program which they might propose to the schools.

Despite these obstacles, Boston enjoys favorable and constructive relationships with individual professors and university centers for a variety of projects ranging from new course development to in-service training and program evaluation. Boston school officials regretted the disappearance of the Harvard-Boston summer school training program for urban teachers and the Boston State program for teachers in disadvantaged areas.

Urban educators report that universities and colleges are needed for:

- Teacher training, provided the trainers have some urban experience and prepare the potential teacher for the reality of an urban classroom
- Evaluation assistance, as rigorous and professional as resources permit and guidelines require
- Feedback on research, with constructive criticism directed first to school officials
- Assistance in planning for and solving future educational, medical, mental health, legal, and social problems
- Ideas on curriculum development, special education, and specific subject matter, such as reading.

Universities, to serve the needs of the urban child, must:

- Recruit experienced urban educators with big city backgrounds to work with the idealistic and more theoretical instructors who staff many teacher training programs
- Allow college sophomores and juniors to work in the schools as tutors, aides and volunteers for credit, and to participate in at least limited practice teaching (as Yale students have done)
- Encourage professional leaves during which academics could exchange roles with urban classroom teachers and administrators for periods ranging from one week to a semester or year

- Insist on the dissemination of urban school research to the teachers and school system otherwise "exploited" by experimentation, surveys or field research for dissertations or larger team projects
- Offer opportunities for talented city teachers and administrators to assist in teacher and administrator training as partners and members of the faculty
- Co-sponsor in-service courses given at times convenient to teachers and other staff.

City school officials, at the same time, must:

- Treat deans not as men who can command and direct faculty as subordinates but as administrators of independent centers and clusters of potential trainers, evaluators, consultants, and researchers
- Vigorously accept and exchange criticism and question the *status quo*
- Exploit the rivalry and competitiveness of area colleges and universities by inviting alternative proposals for training, research, planning and evaluation tasks
- Insist on final reports to school officials and parents and summary consultation as one price for research in and on schools or projects in the system
- Issue periodic "report cards" on the quality of teachers and other staff prepared by colleges and universities

The system should reestablish the kind of school system—university forum which gave school officials and university representatives a chance to discuss mutual criticisms. The Boston School Department should include in this forum representatives from the university other than the schools of education—the medical schools, the law schools, the schools of social work and of public health, the Sloan School of Management, MIT and Harvard Business Schools, and other centers and institutes concerned about the city, young people, and the flow of social services to urban populations.

The Schools and Other Agencies

Schools must work in cooperation with other government agencies. They share their clients with other departments—for example, many of the functions of health and recreation overlap. At the same time, other municipal departments like the Public Facilities Department, the Law Department, and the Office of Human Rights include the Boston School Department among their clients and collaborators.

Boston Redevelopment Authority and
Public Facilities Department

Boston has at least two agencies in addition to the Educational Planning Center of the school department which have major responsibilities for planning school facilities. These are the Boston Redevelopment Authority and the Public Facilities Department. The latter is a relatively new agency created to replace the moribund school construction department.

The BRA has helped plan new schools by sponsoring the Sargent Study of School Facilities Needs in 1963 and by assisting on other projects, notably the planning of the Campus High the Sargent study recommended. For three years, officials debated the site location. Between 1967 and 1969, the Campus High proposal was buried as a low priority item on the list of federal funds. Land acquisition has been so painfully slow that in 1970 fewer than five acres were available for the first stage of a 5,000 pupil Campus High School.

Campus High was to be the keystone of a senior high-middle or intermediate school program for Boston. Federal funds have dried up—after years of delay. Now, the outlook for a racially balanced central city high school is not good. The BRA was the crucial agency in both planning (most of it has been done) and land acquisition. School officials report that in other cases, relations with the BRA for land-taking and coordinating new schools have been generally satisfactory, especially under the present BRA director.

The Public Facilities Department now constructs public buildings in Boston. A three-man commission supervises and guides the work of the PFD staff. The superintendent of schools currently sits as one commissioner. Another member, the deputy mayor, is a Boston school principal on leave. The third is a member of the mayor's staff. So the schools, in addition to contract provisions which require that the superintendent approve school plans at several critical points are well-represented in the process.

Two new school buildings, the William Monroe Trotter School and the Hastings Street School, opened in September 1969. A dozen new schools opened in 1971 and 1972. A new secondary school building has been built behind the present English High School. Moreover, some of the new plans are truly innovative—for example, the plan to place a school in an office building where space could be increased or decreased as needed. Other facilities have been leased on an interim basis and skillfully remodeled. The Boston High School on Newbury Street bears no physical resemblance to the garage it once was.

The PFD has also supported the idea of a downtown high school (which would be part of the Model Subsystem) to develop new ways to educate senior high students. This school would include a base downtown from which students would go to study in cultural centers, firms, museums, public agencies, hospitals, and a variety of adult settings—at potentially great savings in school plant.

New schools have been planned and should be constructed as rapidly as possible. Adoption of the new building codes (the Eisenberg Report) should make construction more economical. The Boston School Committee and Public Facilities Department share a common interest in the code that emphasizes performance standards rather than old-fashioned construction techniques.

Gradually both the PFD and the Boston school system educational planning staff have invested more time in community liaison work. But communities need considerable exposure to new ideas in education before they understand and accept some of the new features of school construction—from divisible spaces to open-plan buildings. The most interested and creative citizens in each neighborhood or group of communities should be consulted and involved in matters of selection of the site and architect, program specifications, and special facilities for community use.

In spite of the problems inherent in community involvement, several departments have discovered that they must work with a responsible cross-section of the community as well as with teachers and principals on new school proposals.

Recommendations

- The BRA, the mayor and the council must place a much higher priority on land acquisition for secondary school facilities—especially for Campus High, the Occupational Resource Center, and other sites near or part of redevelopment areas.
- The PFD should continue to include the superintendent of schools or a senior representative in charge of planning on the commission and should periodically review relationships and issue public reports on the status of school construction projects.
- The city should adopt the new building code proposals as soon as possible, saving hundreds of thousands of dollars and eliminating the needless waste of expensive building materials.
- Communities should not only be consulted but should continue their involvement in an advisory capacity as part of the planning and construction process. This involvement should consist of special citizen committees contributing from the time of site search to opening day—as is common practice in suburbs and smaller cities.

The Law Department

The Corporation Counsel presently provides legal services to the Boston School Department, because the department cannot retain an attorney of its own. Recently, the number of school contracts has increased because of federal programs and the need for outside evaluation and consultation. Student and parent litigation has increased, as have teacher requests for court rulings on their rights.

For collective bargaining, however, the school committee retains a labor relations consultant, an attorney who has been on the National Labor Relations Board staff and has been involved in other school bargaining cases.

The business manager's office must prepare much of the data for contracts with vendors and individuals. Many contracts are delayed for months until Law Department staff can find time to complete work on school business. The contract for this study, only ($10,000 from the city), required more than six months of negotiation and paper work.

At one point, when the study was almost completed, the contract still had not been signed. Dr. Cyril Sargent, the major author of two reports on Boston school facilities (one in the early 1950s, another in the early 1960s) observed that this characterized his experience with other city agencies and the Law Department at that time.

The Corporation Counsel recognizes the problem and reports substantial increases in staff time for all city legal business. More than one attorney has been made available for school concerns. One of them has been helpful to the superintendents and principals in disputes over pupil rights and helped conduct an in-service workshop on that topic. Some others have been less effective—e.g., in handling the court injunction proceedings before a strike or in expediting contracts.

The advantages of drawing on the city Law Department include the factor of specialization, for the department has experts on legislation, business contracts, damage suits, pupil rights. The disadvantages include a discontinuity in service as attorneys change assignments and delays as a result of overload assignments.

Several large city departments like Boston City Hospital and the Police Department have a Law Department attorney in residence who works full time on the priorities of that department.

Recommendations

- The Boston School Department should have one or more attorneys. The school department should select the lawyer (as is done in many large city school systems), or at least have him or her attached to the school system, with a desk at school headquarters.
- Law Department specialists should continue to be used not only for contracts and cases, but also for the briefing of school officials on emerging legal problems which affect student, parent, and teacher civil rights.
- Every effort should be made to expedite school contracts and other business, for delays in these tend to undermine confidence in municipal administration and convey minimal concern for the education of children in Boston.

Park and Recreation Department

The school and park departments have many facilities, both indoor and outdoor, which could be shared with the schools. In addition to school buildings, the school committee has authority over the George Robert White Stadium, which is used for track, football, and other events.

Individual members of the school committee have shown a deep interest in park and recreation programs and facilities. Nevertheless, rules and restrictions have made it difficult for school officials and park officials to coordinate the use of facilities.

Progress has been made recently. The White Stadium is now open for games and meets that the city organizes in summer and after-school programs. High school teams now use the Franklin Park Golf Course more often. The city has repaired a number of tennis courts and recently opened a major new tennis facility. Evening baseball games are now possible, according to the director of physical education for the school department.

The park commissioner for the city of Boston has advanced ideas for recreation programs for the elderly, for girls, and for the handicapped, as well as for the expansion of existing athletic programs. Special education officials have begun using skating rinks and co-sponsoring junior olympic meets for handicapped children.

The school department has explored the possibility of using facilities that are otherwise used very little during the day: boys' club gyms, YMCA pools, and the Arena Annex. The need for using these facilities is especially urgent in the older sections of the city where playgrounds and recreational facilities are scarce and population density very high.

Boston cannot afford duplication of facilities either with the separate departments or with the M.D.C. which has built hockey rinks and playgrounds in various parts of the city.

Recommendations

- The city needs a park and recreation council which would bring together for mutual planning and discussion representatives of the Boston School Department, Boston Parks and Recreation Department, the Metropolitan District Commission, and private agencies concerned about recreation, e.g., YMCA, YWCA, Boys Clubs, etc. The Physical Education Department would be the permanent member but would be joined as the agenda required by representatives of special education, adult education, and of the custodians.
- The school department and the city must develop ways to prorate and share costs for community recreation—dances, fairs and festivals. Sumerthing, athletic clinics, and other uses—not just in new community schools but in existing buildings as well. The city's recreation needs are diverse, and too many of its public facilities close at 4:45 P.M.
- Some facilities can be decentralized. The school committee must join in planning improved fields and facilities in East Boston, Brighton, Charlestown,

West Roxbury and Hyde Park. Where it is possible, these facilities should be adjacent to junior high and senior high schools.

New ideas should be actively solicited and creative new facilities in other cities visited and studied.

The Mayor's Office of Human Rights

In recent years many large cities have established human rights or human relations commissions to deal with the special problems minority groups have in finding decent housing and jobs; Boston has established the Mayor's Office of Human Rights.

Relations between the school department and the mayor's office have been good, especially in times of conflict. In 1970 the director of the office was an attorney who had taught for three years in a predominantly black junior high school. He worked closely with school staff to resolve disputes and to avert serious trouble at Hyde Park High, English High, and other schools.

This office is particularly concerned about schools because racial conflict, if not handled skillfully, tends to spill into the streets and neighborhoods. So far, Boston's record, although not without problems, is better than those of many other cities where some secondary schools have become armed camps with police on duty in the school and aides at every door.

The major problem in Boston is that many principals are untrained to deal with racial strife, student demands, and problem-solving in general—all of which are essential when a community is boiling over with resentment at conditions in the schools.

Principals must show evidence of training and of performance in working with multiracial faculties, student groups, and communities before selection. Success in working with diverse groups should be given priority above test scores and interviews when the school department selects candidates for promotion.

Also, parents in the community should be involved in defining the criteria for principals in their neighborhoods and in interviewing candidates so that principals can be assigned to schools where their talents are appropriate and acknowledged.

While he is working, a principal must get continuing assistance, advice, and training in community relations skills. This training can be planned in cooperation with the Office of Human Rights and the staffs of Little City Halls.

Since 1964 a dozen large cities have applied for funds under various federal programs (especially under Title IV of the Civil Rights Act of 1964). These funds would be used to develop capacities for improved intergroup relations. The local record, at least in promoting school integration, is not especially strong. The Boston school system has missed the opportunity seized by other school systems. Of course, first the rating system should change according to suggestions in the deans' study. According to the present rating system, candidates for the office would have to be selected only from within the system.

Recommendations

- The Office of Human Rights should continue to assist in school problems as it is needed. It should be involved in plans for in-service training of principals and other staff.
- Periodically, staff members of the OHR should be invited to meetings of area superintendents and principals so that they can review policies and discuss preventative measures and constructive programs in education.
- Each area superintendent should have an assistant to work with him and with area principals to foster better school-community relationships (see the section, "area superintendents" in Chapter 3). The assistant would often be an assistant principal and his work would be part of his advanced training in community leadership as preparation for the principalship.

Model Cities

Boston was one of the first cities in the country to receive funds under the Model Cities program, a program designed to improve the quality of urban life in selected neighborhoods and provide models for entire cities.

Only three of the many Model Cities programs in Boston directly concern the public schools, and these illustrate varied approaches. The largest of the three is the School-Community Communication Program (SCCP), intended to organize and to train parents to more effectively seek improvements in educational quality.

The SCCP includes a neighborhood worker in each of the six areas of the Boston Model Neighborhood, and an administrative staff working directly under the Model Neighborhood Board. The program staff must identify issues on which teachers, administrators, and parents can collaborate to produce results, and develop organizing strategies that sustain parents' interest.

The SCCP's stated purpose reflects a concern shared by many inner-city principals and other school staff: how to bring about informed parental involvement in educational matters. Participants in the workshop on School-Community Relations, which was part of this study, spent much time searching for solutions. The SCCP could be an instrument to educate parents and to help them translate their concerns into results, particularly if it operates "in close cooperation with the Boston School Department."

An example of how the SCCP can begin to meet the need for communication occurred during the summer of 1970. Activist parents in one area decided that the local Home and School Association, under newly-elected leadership which represented the three major ethnic groups in the area, had great potential for improving the local schools. They asked that the SCCP work to strengthen the Home and School Association. As a result, two of its officers were put on the SCCP staff for a month.

In this situation, the Home and School Association could serve as an advisory council. In other areas the SCCP staff found that the Home and School Association had a reputation for passivity and that parents were demanding a more effective and independent organization.

The SCCP program is funded by the Department of Housing and Urban Development. Its budget for fiscal year 1970-71 was projected at $111,815.

Recommendations

- The SCCP is directed, at least nominally, by a planning committee of neighborhood and agency representatives. The area superintendents should serve on or be represented on this planning committee. It is to the school's advantage that the SCCP *work*.
- Principals and members of their staffs should meet on a regular basis with the SCCP organizers assigned to their areas. Community organizers need to be educated about the school system; in turn, the organizers can teach much about what is going on in the community.
- Principals should help SCCP organizers identify issues on which the organizers could obtain results with relative ease. It is vital that the SCCP be successful at the outset. Among these issues might be organizing a school library or a School Volunteers project. Principals should not expect the organizers to limit themselves to safe issues, however; they should be prepared to deal with substantive demands.
- Principals are entitled to proof that a particular demand reflects many parents' concern. A mechanism for holding referenda for parents on specific issues could remove much of the tension in school-community relations.

The Increased Local Educational
Responsibility Program

The ILERP is the planning arm of the Model Cities program for the schools. Model Cities Administration planners, in connection with the Racial Imbalance Law, have developed a comprehensive plan for new schools in the Model Cities area. The Model Cities plan is based on the partnership concept of pairing predominantly black and predominantly white schools through shared programs at a common resource center:

Unlike the open enrollment system on which the Trotter School "magnet" concept is based, partnership schools do not require that children be removed from their neighborhood environment and travel as individuals to another school every day. On the contrary, the partnership system depends on the home school as a strongly community-oriented base from which children in groups venture forth into new territory. Resource centers are places where groups meet as equals, not an environment which is defined as "belonging" to anyone.

The State Racial Imbalance Task Force and the Boston School Committee have given a qualified endorsement to the partnership approach to planning new schools in Boston. Many difficulties must be worked out before this approach can be successful.

Many benefits could result from this innovative program. Children would learn in an environment enriched not only by racial diversity, but also by close association with a major museum or other cultural institution. Teachers would be given opportunities to use new approaches and to work closely with colleagues who have a variety of skills. The taxpayer in Boston would benefit because the state assumes 65 percent of the construction costs of racially-balanced schools, which in this case would include the new schools built in predominantly black neighborhoods.

The projected cost of this program, including the pilot project, is $325,635; planning is projected to cost $75,635.

Recommendations

- A working committee of Model Cities Administration ˙staff and school department staff should be formed immediately to work through the problems hampering a pilot project.
- Top level administrators in the school department should give priority to implementing the working committee's recommendations.
- The Boston school department and the Public Facilities Department should analyze the impact on the city's total construction plan of up to twelve schools which might be built using the partnership plan. They should seek funds for this analysis from the State Department of Education's Bureau of School Building Assistance. The analysis should include a study of the impact of demographic changes and of possible parochial school closings.
- A working committee representing the school department, the PFD, the BRA, the State Department of Education's Bureau of School Building Assistance, and those public agencies offering health, guidance, and recreational services should develop plans for coordinated use of school buildings.
- This planning should assure that new school facilities can serve as centers to deliver varied services. The Model Cities Administration should see that such services are coordinated and delivered to provide maximum benefit to clients.

- This approach would require legislative action to reimburse local agencies for constructing facilities to be used for purposes other than education.

The Program for Children with Special Learning Problems

This program is a significant attempt to coordinate the resources of the Model Cities Administration, the Boston School Department, and an outside agency to meet the needs of a group of children.

Its purpose is to help schools and other agencies meet more adequately the needs of children who have neurological or emotional learning disabilities. The school department and the program staff have conducted a study of programs for children with learning problems; a number of parents have also been involved in planning.

The major focus of the second year will be to establish special demonstration classes at the Dearborn School to provide training opportunities for professional and nonprofessional staff. Extensive outreach services will be part of this pilot project.

The Boston University-Boston City Hospital Child Guidance Clinic is working closely with this project, providing the kind of technical expertise the school department cannot and should not have to provide.

The Program for Children with Learning Problems was funded for 1970-71 at the level of $31,360. This does not include the cost of the pilot project at the Dearborn School, for which the school department would have to seek additional funds.

14 The Boston School Committee

A five-man elected school committee has governed the Boston Public Schools since 1906. During the previous century the committee fairly often changed in size, structure, and function. At one point, the committee had as many as seventy-six elected members, six from each ward. After 1875 the mayor chaired a committee of twenty-five. The legislature relieved the mayor of the chairmanship in 1885, when the first Irish-born Mayor of Boston took office.

The 1906 changes occurred as a result of a campaign by the Boston banker and attorney, James Jackson Storrow. Storrow had been frustrated by his experiences on the large Boston School Committee whose subcommittees made key decisions about education and hiring staff. He asked Harvard professor Paul Hanus to survey other large cities, many of which had reduced the size of their school boards as part of a general reform movement to eliminate patronage, corruption, and inefficiency. Hanus, his Harvard colleague Henry Holmes, and Storrow prepared for the legislature a bill to establish a committee of from three to seven citizens whom the mayor would appoint. Dozens of civic leaders, including former mayors and Louis Brandeis, endorsed the plan. Women voters, however, asked to restore the idea of an elective board since they had fought to win the right to vote for school committee.

The smaller elected at-large school committee passed, with the idea of a stronger superintendency, board of superintendents, and business agent. The superintendent won the right to nominate all teachers and principals. The committee appointed the top officers and all nonacademic personnel.

Not until 1944 was the system challenged. George D. Strayer, a Columbia University professor, directed a study team which recommended an appointed board whose members would be ratified by the voters the year after they served. The mayor would select from names suggested by a group of college presidents, civic and professional leaders. The legislature did not adopt the recommendations.

During the 1960s various groups proposed once again some form of appointive board. The American Jewish Committee, Catholic Interracial Committee, and other groups concerned with minority representation on a governing board supported the idea.

Most recently the mayor of Boston has recommended an appointive board, as has the Home Rule Charter Study Commission, which in 1969-1970 worked on ways to streamline and decentralize city government in Boston.

What is the evidence on appointive versus elective boards? There is no compelling evidence that either one is more effective in solving educational problems or in saving money. One research study suggests that an appointive board is slightly more effective at getting bond issues passed. Another study finds that appointed boards are more likely to conduct national searches for superintendents and select those who have held other city superintendencies more often, but there are some exceptions to this. A survey research team at the University of Chicago found that appointive boards more readily responded to requests to make policy declarations toward eliminating *de facto* segregation in schools. But no major city has been able to transform a favorable policy statement into reality when large numbers of white citizens refuse to given their consent. It would appear that an appointive board might have several advantages in search for funds and outside talent and in establishing integration policies.

But the appointive board takes power away from the people and gives it to the mayor or some other elective official. Often, a mayor appoints his friends or supporters unless prominent officials of various civic and professional groups advise him to do otherwise. This advice by a panel or special nominating commission is what Chicago and Philadelphia use (and New York City until the late 1960s). The Strayer Report suggested a similar plan for Boston.

The current study and several Becker polls in 1969 and 1970 indicate that the Boston electorate in general supports the idea of an elective school committee. However, Boston has the smallest school committee of any of the large city school systems in the United States, smaller even than those of several middle-sized Massachusetts communities (e.g., Lowell, Newton, Brockton) which have six or more members.[a] The 1906 reform swung the pendulum too far in the direction of governance by a very small group. Boston in the nineteenth century governed the schools with larger committees.

A five-member committee has some advantages—compact size, economy in terms of assistants and office space, ample time for each member to speak and be heard. Its disadvantages are that the committee cannot reflect the city's diversity earlier committees (chosen by wards) could, or even as the city council can. As a result, the school committee includes members from fewer sections of the city than does the city council. The small committee also does not reflect a diversity of talents and experience.

The study team examined different sizes of committees from five to fifteen (the size of the Pittsburgh School Board in a similarly sized city). The staff also considered the idea of election by wards or by clusters of wards or sections of the city.

Does a city need a separate board of education at all? The time may come when communities do not use a separate school board, preferring to use a state-wide or metropolitan system with all funds from state and federal taxes. A local board may then be strictly advisory. But in New England, popular control

---

[a]In Massachusetts cities more than half of the school committees have seven members and a majority of the remainder have nine or ten.

of education is a valuable tradition. It should not be discarded lightly, at least while money is raised by the city property tax.

The diversity of a city should be reflected by the composition of a school committee. In Boston, several sections of the city are rarely if ever represented by members residing there. East Boston, Roxbury, the South End, and Allston-Brighton rarely have a member elected. The members elected at large do try to represent each area of the city. They attend graduations, listen to citizen complaints, and even schedule school committee meetings in various sections of the city.

The study team offers this proposal: a nine man school committee made up of Boston residents, eighteen years or older, selected as follows.

First, six members should be elected on a district or area basis, one for each administrative area of the city (with some changes in area boundaries). One of several possible district plans might be: (1) Jamaica Plain, Roslindale, West Roxbury; (2) Allston, Brighton, Back Bay, Beacon Hill; (3) South End-Roxbury; (4) Charlestown, East Boston, Boston Downtown, South Boston; (5) Dorchester; and (6) Hyde Park, Mattapan.

As population shifts, the city should revise area boundary lines. No area should exceed any other in size by more than 10 percent of the total population. Many high schools and some other schools may serve the population of more than one district, and thus require city-wide members of the school committee and parent representation rather than geographical representation on school and area councils.

Second, three members should be either elected at large, or if testimony at the home rule hearings indicates, appointed by the mayor with the consent of the city council and on the basis of recommendations from ten civic leaders who shall transmit to the mayor twice as many names as exist vacancies. The civic leaders should include the presidents of the County Bar Association, Boston Chamber of Commerce, Medical Society, Boston League of Women Voters, Boston Central Labor Council, Home and School Association, Community Service Association, and heads of three local universities or colleges accredited by a regional association. These executives, or their designated representatives, must maintain residences in Boston. The appointive method ought to make possible the selection of several women, one student, and members of minority groups with little electoral strength at the polls.

Terms

The two-year term requires a school committeeman to be as responsive as a U.S. Congressman, whose concern for reelection often takes up much of his time. The study staff proposes a four-year term for district school committee members coterminous with the mayor's term, thereby ensuring that district members would be selected when voter turnout is relatively heavy. The at-large members would be selected for four-year terms when city council elections are held.

Signature Requirements

Currently a candidate for school committee must collect 2,000 signatures during the middle of the summer, a difficult time to attract workers and supporters. Under the new committee plan a district candidate would need 300 signatures. If the at-large members are elected, they would need 1,000.

Staff Assistance and Compensation

The nine members would require secretarial assistance on a half-time basis, full-time for the chairman only. The secretary of the school committee would supervise five secretaries selected from the civil service lists or from present employees; these nine would work with the school committee.

Each member would receive $500 a month for each month the committee held a minimum of two meetings. This would compensate for loss of income and expenses incurred, and make it possible for less wealthy individuals to serve. It would also eliminate the committee's reliance on fund-raising events such as testimonial dinners each year, "birthday parties," and other festivities where tickets are sold to or by school department employees. This practice makes committee members unduly dependent on certain categories of employees who sell many tickets or feel they must contribute to maintain their salary position, a stituation which undermines the collective bargaining process and leads to charges of favoritism at promotion time.

In fact, a state law should be passed which makes it illegal for school committee members to receive campaign contributions or "birthday" gifts from school department employees. Boston schools need a local Hatch Act to protect employees and school committee members who find it objectionable to have tickets pawned off on the staff for annual fund-raisers.

Each committee member would also be available on at least two other days per month to conduct hearings on problems in his area. The member should chair a hearing panel with the area superintendent, a teacher representative, one or more parents, one or more students—whoever the area council designates in its annual meeting. In most cases the council would advise the area superintendent who would ordinarily take action or, if the matter were controversial, refer it to the superintendent and school committee for a policy decision. This process could ease the burden on the central committee, speed up the process of getting a hearing, and provide a response based on the people's needs in each section of the city.

**The Flow of Reports and Information
to the Boston School Committee**

How does a school committee member learn about a problem? Where does he get the facts? How does he decide what problems deserve higher priority than others? What information does he get from the staff? How does information flow from citizens, teachers, and principals to the school committee? Does the information come in time and in the right form to allow a prompt decision?

A grant from the Danforth Foundation made it possible for members of the study staff to attend almost all the school committee meetings from October 1967 through October 1969. The meetings were analyzed to determine what kinds of decisions the school committee made and with what data. Certain patterns emerged.

First, the first and second items on almost every agenda are: personnel—academic; and personnel—nonacademic.

The associate superintendent of personnel, working with the secretary of the school committee and his own staff, prepares for each meeting abundant background materials on all personnel appointments, professional and nonprofessional, and on transfers, requests for leave, and retirements. Rated lists of candidates for promotion appear at intervals. With promotions, the number of points each candidate has earned appears on a list in rank order.

Since the late 1940s, associate and assistant superintendents have been nominated by the superintendent of schools at a school committee meeting.

Personnel items occupy the greatest space on the school committee's agendas and most of the space in the committee's official proceedings. The first and most popular items on the agenda appear to be about employment of adults by the system. The information available to the committee is detailed and generally clear. The committee usually takes action promptly; occasionally it holds an item over for a week or two at the request of a member who wants more information (or has an alternative candidate).

Second, the school committee reacts to the deadlines of other local, state, and federal agencies.

Each year the staff—primarily the directors, the board of superintendents and especially the business manager—prepares a preliminary budget. In January, the school committee reviews the budget, suggests any additions or deletions, and sends it to the mayor for review. By early April the committee must review and adjust the budget again within the limits set by the mayor and the statute.

The business manager has prepared the information in different formats at various times. Sometimes the format includes specific data on the money each school and school district needs. It always uses the line item format to indicate how many positions in each category will be filled and how much equipment and materials will be purchased.

State and federal agencies require another set of deadlines according to the project and the availability of funds. Examples include the various titles (categories) of the Elementary and Secondary Education Act, Vocation Education grants, the Education Professions Development Act, and many more. Primarily because of the federal appropriations cycle (action usually comes late in the year), funding under these federal statistics does not often coincide with the budget timetable.

The Racial Imbalance Act sets another deadline. It requires an October 1 racial census, a report, and later, a plan of action which includes short- and long-range steps to reduce and to eliminate imbalance. The committee and staff must supply the statistical data required under the statute.

Committee members find the budget information accurate. Some of them wish there could be more evaluation data on programs that are working well—information beyond school system officials' testimony. School committeemen in Boston have not yet insisted on a program budget that puts a price tag on the total cost of various programs (e.g., remedial reading, secondary school social studies, athletics) including cost of teachers, materials, and textbooks. Nor has there been a demand for a program budget that includes an evaluation of *alternatives* (with the cost of each alternative matched with its effectiveness or benefits).

Committee members complain about many of the state and federal programs. Often they find a proposal must be read, approved, and signed right away to meet a federal agency deadline. The committee lacks time to consider alternatives; they are rarely offered choices. Frequently the staff must act quickly because of changing federal requirements (extra money is suddenly available, or guidelines are issued only two weeks before the deadline).

Committee members have had sufficient time to discuss the imbalance statistics and the school building plans which are reviewed at least once a year and revised according to shifts in school enrollment.

Third, collective negotiations with employee groups require frequent progress reports from school committee negotiators.

The teacher contract is only one of seven employee contracts. The school committee hires a full-time coordinator and a part-time labor relations counsel who conduct the negotiations. In each instance they inform the committee of initial demands for improved salaries and working conditions, and they receive the committee's instructions, usually in executive sessions.

Legally teachers' salaries cannot be raised after September 1. More realistically, the school committee should make salary decisions by the first Monday in April, the budget deadline. Although the teachers' union indicated a desire to meet this April deadline, a negotiations impasse continued not only after the deadline, but also after a major strike.

The problem seems not to be one of information, but rather of timing the decision to be part of the budgetary process. Salaries account for more than 80 percent of total school allocations each year and 90 percent of instruction costs.

Fourth, the committee receives requests for hearings from various employee and community groups.

Employee groups can request hearings to present salary requests or to reach the final step in the grievance process. Community groups can request a hearing through the secretary of the school committee, the chairman, or an individual member. Any member can place a request for a hearing on the agenda.

The committee's record as a hearing board is uneven. Some groups get a quick response. Other groups, like the Lewenberg parents, may be granted a closed hearing only after months of postponement and delay. Some groups are denied hearings on the grounds that their request or concern has been dealt with administratively.

The committee has met frequently with representatives of the King-Timilty Council about federal grants, personnel matters, and other specialized concerns. It has met with parents from Allston, Mattapan, and other sections of the city about facilities and personnel matters.

The committee has conducted as many as four meetings a year in various sections of the city, from East Boston to Hyde Park and Roxbury, for parents and citizens whose testimony they have welcomed. Teachers, students, and state representatives have addressed the committee at some of these forums on problems ranging from airplane noise to corporal punishment.

As an unpaid board, committee members find it difficult at times to meet on the scheduled day or to grant all requests for hearings. Nor can they visit all sections of the city each year and still transact their routine business. Nor are hearings the only way to gather information—although they are interesting, and allow committee members to judge the intensity of local feelings.

Fifth, the committee approves textbooks and courses of study.

Traditionally and by statute, the committee reviews all texts, regular and supplementary, and course of study guides that teachers use. Staff committees conduct the initial screening of materials; they then make the books and materials available to school committee members so they can review them.

This review of instructional materials consumes much of their time. Often only one former member looked at all the materials, although others do try to examine potentially controversial materials.

This procedure has origins in the seventeenth century when ministers and other educated men examined teachers, books, and students. No longer does the committee worry about religious orthodoxy, but the school staff members ought to worry about what biology texts might include or which authors can be quoted in courses on minority groups.

Ironically, the newer media like films, filmstrips, and programmed instruction are even more difficult for a committee of laymen to review. Books are still the staple, but students now learn as much if not more from other modes of instruction.

The greatest obstacle to meeting the diverse needs of a complex system may be the pattern of one course guide for each subject. In many areas—science, English, and social studies—a variety of course guides might better serve the needs of a diverse population. Or perhaps a course guide is less useful to teachers and children in many subjects than would be an evaluation of alternative materials from which a class might select. If the latter is true, then the traditional flow of materials to be approved may be obsolete even though it is required of the school committee.

Sixth, an incredible array of problems comes before the school committee— requests for out-of-state travel by staff, permission to maintain a tavern within so many yards of a school building, problems of athlete eligibility in league competition, and new ventures like the Model Cities proposals which carried implications for the schools.

These are formal established activities. In addition, the committee can and does solicit information and advice from the superintendent, the board of superintendents, the chief schoolhouse custodian, and others who regularly attend school committee meetings. The committee may seek information from the chief structural engineer or from any of the nearly three dozen directors of departments.

Informally, the committee members learn of problems and decision opportunities in many other ways.

Each member has a secretary or staff assistant whose salary in 1970 was $9,991.80. This assistant handles many requests for information and assistance. The requests he receives range from information on vacant seats so that parents can take advantage of open enrollment to requests for assistance in getting a teaching or secretarial job in the school department. The latter type of request ought to be handled by personnel officials despite a long Boston tradition of using elected officials to help one get a job.

Dozens of reports come to the school committee's attention. The Educational Planning Center staff conducts special studies in areas like facility needs and site locations and the best way to establish a new department—for example, one for research and evaluation. External sources for reports include federal agencies, the Massachusetts Advisory Council on Education, Massachusetts Department of Education and ABCD (Agency for Boston Community Development). A former school committee member commented it was impossible to digest all the reports; he gave many of them to newspaper reporters on the condition that they give him a written summary he could examine. Other reports include evaluations of federal programs, some with statistics and tables that lay citizens are not trained to comprehend.

The mass media, especially newspapers and television, bring many issues to the surface and indirectly create much of the criticism and much of the support the committee receives. The media tend to play up conflict, school walkouts, the teachers' strike of 1970, high school accreditation decisions, school fires, and reports that criticize the system. The committee reaction appears to be ambivalent; members resent the stress on problems and protest instead of on progress. But they do like the public visibility that controversy generates. Recently staff members have been added to the committee to present additional information to the public and to school department employees about new programs and triumphs, scholastic and athletic.

Court suits, often a new source of guidelines, increasingly indicate to the school committee and other school officials a need to reexamine school department policies. Recently litigants have challenged the continued use of corporal punishment; the right to fire nontenured teachers without a hearing; the necessity for girls to score higher on Latin School admission tests than boys; the school committee's right to substitute its nominee for the superintendent's nominee; the equity of special education testing and evaluation procedures, and other practices. Parents and students will continue to seek clarification of their civil rights to information, to protection from arbitrary action, to admission to programs made available to others (e.g., through tests or tracking). In this domain, the committee—although most of the members are attorneys—relies heavily on the Law Department counsel.

These formal and informal inputs are not all of the school committee's information sources. It learns of some problems through citizen phone calls, through discussions with parents at school graduations or at social gatherings, and through an annual review of legislative proposals that might affect the Boston schools.

But how adequate are the existing procedures? Reviewing the evidence suggests that the Boston School Committee gets the most information and expends the greatest effort on personnel or employment matters—from hiring and transfer decisions to collective bargaining. On these matters, the staff provides ample materials.

The committee gets less information on the evaluation of the total educational program—federal programs are a possible exception. But even on federal programs, the committee does not review and select among alternative proposals; it finds it must generally decide whether or not to expand an existing program. Federal, state, and local officials may need a rapid decision, a situation which prevents the committee from making a full, searching review of the program and its alternatives. On the other hand, committee members often ask a great many questions about the consultants hired to assist with training or evaluation of federal and other programs. They often hold consultant contracts for further study, a feature related more to questions of who gets the contract than to education program review.

As a hearing board, the committee serves an important function as a last resort. At the same time, many problems concerning personnel—including the transfer of ineffective or inappropriate principals—should never get to the school committee; they could be resolved administratively. Because citizens and employees need councils where their voices are heard, some of these councils should be much closer to the school site.

The committee generally gets the information it needs to make routine decisions about specific people and specific departments and about the annual cycle of personnel recruitment and selection, the budget, and selection of system-wide texts and courses of study.

But the committee is not served well in coping with school population changes or program changes that new state and federal mandates make possible. Since 1965 the superintendent and staff have developed new ways to identify the need for change, for example, in the dramatic increases in the number of minority group students. The new Office of Curriculum Development, the Bilingual Department, the Educational Planning Center, and the Public Information Office exist in response to the need for new courses, new staff patterns, new facilities, and the explanation of these to the press. But many of the committee's old procedures and preferences seem buried in the cement of tradition. The focus is on employment, not on program evolution, and on reviewing system-wide course materials, not on selecting special materials for the special needs of rapidly expanding minorities—especially the Spanish-speaking groups, blacks, and Chinese.

Given the present patterns, the committee will continue to learn of the more intense problems through litigation and through the mass media. Fundamental remedies go beyond the flow of information and require a more diversified committee, a top staff more representative of the diverse population of the city, and a total reform of personnel and budgetary procedures. As of 1973 the new superintendent achieved the second remedy; the other await committee or mayor and council action.

Recommendations for ways to alleviate these difficulties appear in the sections of this report dealing with program evaluation, the budget, minority recruitment, and school-community relations.

 **15** Financing the Boston
Schools in the
Seventies

The Costs of Education

Even if the Boston School Committee and Massachusetts legislature adopt none of the recommendations in this study, the Boston School Department budget will increase between $8 and $10 million each year (a minimum of $40 million in five years). This projection is based on the effects of inflation, average salary increases, and a normal rate of growth in the system. Based on 1968 final figures, the Boston school budget will rise to $120 million by 1972 (see Table 15-1).

Adopting recommendations for economy can save millions of dollars each year. But much of the saving depends on a hiring freeze in certain categories (doctors, nurses, attendance supervisors, teaching assistant principals) and on using instead health aides and community aides at half the cost. Recommendations for new expenditures will exceed the suggested economies, but these expenditures should make delivery of educational services more effective and efficient.

Many expensive proposals could qualify for state and federal funding if the school department requested partial or full support. For example:

- The teacher grants proposal could cost $600,000 a year but might initially qualify for Title III, ESEA funding.
- The Model Schools/Resource Center proposal could use new or existing schools if the regular budget were supplemented by $100,000 for each area, a total of $600,000. Again, Title III, Title II, and other federal funds would be available for schools whose programs respond to area needs.
- A legislative change in 1970 granted authority to the school department to make alterations in existing buildings. Thus the state and the mayor could authorize $1,000,000 to finance alterations that would allow educational innovations such as team teaching and instruction in open spaces in existing schools.
- Emergency funds should be sought for leasing and altering buildings to provide space for those children affected by parochial school closings. Estimates of the cost vary from $500,000 to $2,000,000 a year depending on timing and state actions.

The school department could seek from three to five million dollars each year from state and federal sources in addition to funds for vocational and technical

Table 15-1
Multiyear Financial Plan of the Boston School System

| | (1968) | | Year | | (1972) |
	0	1	2	3	4
Instructional Programs					
Basic education	39,117,442	42,600,000	46,400,000	50,400,000	54,900,000
Special education	3,450,750	3,760,000	4,080,000	4,440,000	4,840,000
Vocational and business education (other than in basic education)	1,933,350	2,100,000	2,290,000	2,480,000	2,710,000
Compensatory education	5,358,347	5,820,000	6,350,000	6,900,000	7,550,000
Adult education and recreation	212,000	231,000	251,000	273,000	298,000
TOTAL INSTRUCTIONAL PROGRAMS	50,071,889	54,511,000	59,371,000	64,493,000	70,298,000
Instructional Support Programs					
Media	191,150	208,000	226,000	246,000	268,000
Curriculum development	20,000	21,800	23,700	25,800	28,100
Educational investigation and measurement	324,940	353,000	385,000	418,000	456,000
Pupil adjustment counseling	218,660	238,000	260,000	282,000	308,000
Teacher placement	249,550	271,000	295,000	322,000	351,000
Educational planning center	1,106,503	1,210,000	1,320,000	1,430,000	1,560,000
Attendance	446,890	486,000	529,000	575,000	627,000
TOTAL INSTRUCTIONAL SUPPORT PROGRAMS	2,557,693	2,787,800	3,038,700	3,298,800	3,598,100

Pupil Personnel Service Programs				
Guidance and counseling	1,500,000	1,380,000	1,270,000	1,170,000	1,074,000
Health services	1,510,000	1,390,000	1,280,000	1,180,000	1,082,230
Student activities					
TOTAL PUPIL PERSONNEL SERVICE PROGRAMS	3,010,000	2,770,000	2,550,000	2,350,000	2,156,230
General Support Programs					
Central administration	3,460,000	3,180,000	2,930,000	2,680,000	2,467,940
School administration (principals and head masters)	2,280,000	2,080,000	1,920,000	1,760,000	1,620,000
Transportation	732,000	671,000	618,000	567,000	521,878
Food services	3,500,000	3,200,000	2,950,000	2,710,000	2,486,970
Maintenance and operation of plant	8,660,000	7,940,000	7,340,000	6,710,000	6,168,437
Planning and engineering	3,230,000	2,960,000	2,720,000	2,500,000	2,296,834
Capital outlay by public facilities	1,390,000	870,000	745,000	855,000	844,428
Fixed charges	2,960,000	2,720,000	2,500,000	2,300,000	2,108,648
Data processing	372,000	341,000	314,000	288,000	265,240
Statistics	47,700	43,500	40,100	36,800	33,760
TOTAL GENERAL SUPPORT PROGRAMS	26,631,700	24,005,500	22,077,100	20,406,800	18,184,135
Community Service Programs					
General community services	309,000	283,000	261,000	239,000	220,140
TOTAL GENERAL COMMUNITY SERVICE PROGRAMS	309,000	283,000	261,000	239,000	220,140
Miscellaneous Programs					
N.Y.C. (Neighborhood Youth Corps)					
Educational publication and information services	49,000	44,900	41,400	38,000	34,940
TOTAL MISCELLANEOUS PROGRAMS	49,000	44,900	41,400	38,000	34,940
GRAND TOTAL	103,895,800	94,895,200	87,339,200	80,332,600	73,855,027

Table 15-1 (cont.)

Physical Data	Number of Units				
Students					
Kindergarten	15,841	15,999	16,159	16,321	16,484
Elementary	44,901	45,350	45,804	46,262	46,725
Junior high	16,743	16,910	17,079	17,250	17,423
Senior high	21,315	21,528	21,743	21,960	22,180
Postsecondary	794	802	810	818	826
Evening	6,000	6,060	6,121	6,182	6,244
Immigrant	646	652	659	666	673
TOTAL STUDENTS	106,240	107,301	108,375	109,459	110,555
Personnel					
Teachers	4,685	4,732	4,799	4,826	4,874
Administrators	430	434	438	442	446
Other personnel	1,100	1,111	1,122	1,133	1,144
TOTAL PERSONNEL	6,215	6,277	6,339	6,401	6,464
Schools	189	192	193	199	204

education which Boston has already begun to pursue. But the city must make clear its commitment and abandon old trade school programs in favor of modern occupational and career education programs for all races.

Other proposals require school committee action on budget requests:

- Two assistants to each area superintendent, @ $17,000 $204,000
- Assistants to associate superintendents $119,000
- Administrative Development Program (at six per year) $102,000
- School clerks—ten more each year $ 50,000
- Spanish-speaking registrars—ten each year $ 50,000
- Full-time assistant principals—ten more each year (but reduce the number of teaching assistant principals by twenty a year) $150,000
- Health aides and Child Advocates   would replace existing staff

Proposals for an ombudsman (the salary and office initially would cost ($30,000 each year) and the paid school committee ($72,000 each year plus secretaries) would require action by the legislature, mayor and the city council. The state would assume the ombudsman's expenses. Such a plan could also be tried on a three-year trial basis, using federal funds.

Other ideas, for year-round schools, for a longer year for principals, and for a differentiated staff would require change in the teachers' contracts, gradual system expansion and additional staff training. The school department should develop a multiyear financial plan as part of the move to PPBES (Program, Planning, Budgeting, Evaluation System).

The Budget and Possible Savings

Even a simple summary of the budget raises interesting questions about the relation between school system activities, goals, and resources allocation. Budget analysis relates cost distribution throughout the system to the system's overall educational philosophy and particular goals and objectives.

Table 15-1, for example, shows that instructional programs claim 67.90 percent of the budget, instructional support claims 3.35 percent, and general support claims 25.48 percent. Does this distribution correspond to school administrators' priorities? Can they justify this distribution, and might they wish to reconsider it? Questions at this program category level become more pointed and more useful when we have some sort of cost distribution norms. The journal SCHOOL MANAGEMENT indicates that, as of January, 1968, New England schools spent an average 78.98 percent of their budgets for Instruction.[1]

Boston's combined expenditure for instructional programs, instructional support programs and pupil personnel service programs amounts to 74.17 percent of the total budget. Why does Boston deviate from the average by 4.81 percent, especially when the educational problems of a big city school system require a proportionately greater expenditure on instruction? Possibly, Boston's program categories may not parallel the journal's instruction category. Perhaps we have not included all costs for activities like compensatory education. These are possible explanations, but there is at least an equal chance that other, more important factors are response for the deviation.

The general support category provides interesting comparisons. Boston pays only 0.71 percent for transportation, less than one-fourth of the median 4.13 percent in New England. Given that the urban school system's transportation costs naturally are lower than the suburban or rural system's, one might still inquire about the adequacy of Boston's transportation program. Does Boston need to spend 1.46 percent for health services, when the median expenditure is 0.97 percent? Considering urban childrens' special health needs and the cost of medical services in an urban area, could Boston supply good health services for less money? Even with high expenditures, are Boston's health services adequate? Clearly the money spent on doctors and on R.N. salaries is excessive, especially considering the work performed.

Even without norms, the program budget provokes useful questions about school system priorities. Among instructional support programs, for example, curriculum development claims 0.83 percent of the budget, and attendance requires 0.61 percent. Is Boston spending too much for attendance and too little for curriculum development? More specifically, given a ranking of goals and objectives for the category and for each program, how effective is the allocation of funds in the instructional support category? Does the 7.32 percent of the budget that is spent for compensatory education genuinely reflect the numbers of Boston school children who need compensatory education, the importance that the school system places on that need, and the resources required to provide an effective compensatory education program?

Does the 2.62 percent of the budget allocated to vocational and business education bear any relation to the numbers of Boston graduates who enter the work force directly from high school? Does basic education alone (53 percent) provide this group with sufficient training for a career? If not, could the system reallocate funds for vocational and business education more effectively? Finally, school officials might want to redesign the program structure and budget to clarify the effectiveness of allocations in the basic education program toward the specific goals of career training, college preparation, and basic education.

Financial Resources for Boston Schools

The property tax is the most immediate source of revenue for Boston schools. But the Boston property tax base has severe limitations:

- Between 1950 and 1970 the property tax base in Boston increased less than 10 percent although municipal and school costs more than doubled.
- During the same twenty years, the percentage of land exempt from taxes in Boston rose from 33 percent to more than 50 percent; most of the exempt land is used for highways, which benefit all Massachusetts residents, new state and federal office facilities, and other governmental structures. Churches and colleges account for a relatively small percentage of tax-exempt property.
- The Boston tax rate is high by Massachusetts standards (despite low residential assessments). And the actual tax burden on those who own or rent homes is high by national standards. Compared to the local tax burdens on families of four persons in the largest city in each of the fifty states, the tax burden in Boston ranks third from the top. Of the large cities only Newark, New Jersey bears a higher local tax burden. Boston taxes in 1968 were heavier than those of Milwaukee, Philadelphia, Baltimore, New York City, Detroit, Miami, Denver, St. Louis, Cleveland, Los Angeles, Chicago, Houston, and many other cities.

Can Boston contribute more of its financial resources to education? A city can always improve property tax administration. The present Boston administration has begun collecting overdue taxes and reevaluating categories of property.

The city can also press for local sales taxes and city income taxes on residents or on all those who earn money in the city. Local leaders have proposed such taxes but they have not won sufficient approval. Some cities like Philadelphia, and New York City collect as much as $200 per family from local nonproperty taxes, but Massachusetts has not yet encouraged special city taxes. It is not clear that these taxes are equitable in a metropolitan area.

In recent years aid from state and federal sources has greatly influenced the Boston school budget.

The Willis-Harrington Report accused the legislature of "systematically starving" the largest city of school funds. In several steps the state has revised the aid formula and begun using current property valuations. The state share of the Boston budget has risen dramatically in eight years from $4 million to more than $25 million in 1970 and $50 million by 1972.

The federal share of the Boston budget has increased, under various federal statutes, from less than $1 million in 1965 to more than $8 million in 1970.

The study staff calculated that more than 90 percent of the budget increases from 1967 to 1969 were subsidized by new state and federal funds. The city of Boston contributed only a small amount of new money despite the annual battle with mayor and council over budget increases.

State and federal funds carry restrictions and, in many cases, they require specific policies or programs. Many local officials would prefer to receive money with no restrictions on its use. But it can be argued that money earmarked for educationally disadvantaged children, vocational education, planning, bilingual education, and other specific purposes actually provides incentives for rapid response to critical problems.

At the same time, the costs of health, education and welfare services are increasing rapidly and many communities cannot pay for them. Massachusetts has shown leadership in assuming the costs of welfare from hard-pressed cities and towns. The nation is experiencing a revolution in financing comprehensive health care for all persons regardless of income. In education the situation is somewhat different.

First, federal funds for education have actually declined since 1967 when defense expenditures for the Vietnam war escalated. Second, unlike welfare, full state funding of local educational costs would relieve local tax burdens more in some expensive suburbs and small towns than in the cities. Furthermore, many citizens seriously question full state and federal financing of education on the grounds that they will lose local options and local goals.

Nevertheless, the gross national product of the United States will pass the trillion dollar mark (during the 1970s). Both the Democratic and Republican parties agree on the need to share surplus federal revenues with state and local governments.

Federal-state revenue sharing is only one source of funds for local education in Boston and other Massachusetts communities. The state will also be forced to revise the state income tax which taxes the rich at the same percentage rate as lower- and middle-income people.

A majority of Massachusetts voters fear the graduated income tax or the concept of a "blank-check" for state services. They might be more willing to consider using it to pay a greater share of the costs of monitored educational programs.

Many national leaders, among them former High Commissioner James B. Conant, have called for full state financial support of education. Former Massachusetts Commissioner of Education Owen B. Kiernan urges this step for Massachusetts as have several mayors and legislators of both parties. Commissioner Neil V. Sullivan coined the term "educare" and asked for one-third state and one-third federal support of education as a first step.

Equal Opportunity and Local Options

The U.S. Advisory Commission on intergovernmental relations has taken a close look at education and welfare financing. To equalize educational opportunity and reduce the growing pressure on the property tax, the commission called for state assumption "of substantially all fiscal responsibility for financing local schools with opportunity for financial enrichment at the local level and assurance of retention of appropriate local policy-making authority."[2]

The commission noted that New Mexico, North Carolina, Delaware, and Louisiana are close to that goal. Hawaii long ago assumed complete financial responsibility for its schools. Both major political parties in California propose moving toward this goal. The concept of full state financing is therefore, neither novel nor utopian; in the 1970s as many as twenty states could adopt proposals like these using sales tax and income tax sources.

The commission recognizes a need to provide for local enrichment of programs, but it urges a limit on local spending of 10 percent of the state grant to preserve the values of equal opportunity and property tax relief. It has drafted suggested state legislation for substantial state financing of schools with local control and the 10 percent local option.

The assumption of substantially all (or at least 90 percent) of the financing for local education in Massachusetts may depend on voter approval of the graduated income tax on the state ballot in 1976. This would be the most equitable tax if it were properly administered. Voters did not approve this tax in 1962, 1968 or 1972. Meanwhile, the property tax burden has continued to rise. State aid to education did rise as a result of the sales tax, although that tax has not offset the effects of inflation and collective bargaining on local property tax rates. The income tax base, unlike the property tax base, increases with inflation; incomes which increase most are taxed appropriately whether or not they invest in property.

Congressional action on federal revenue sharing with a mandatory "pass through" of funds for local services will also have an effect in Boston. Federal tax-sharing and greater use of state income tax powers may help in the mid- and late-1970s. The Nixon administration estimates that the 1975 Boston share should be at least 10 million dollars. Other congressional proposals would yield even more.

For several years, New York has recognized the cities' special needs and offered them "urban aid" for education. Massachusetts, to its credit, was one of only three states to invest in compensatory education for disadvantaged children before 1965. But since that time the major new funds for education have come from Federal sources, (with gradual reductions in appropriations each year). State aid to municipalities must increase both for annual school operations and for other municipal services such as health and transportation.

As of 1970 Boston spent more than $700 to instruct each child compared to over $1300 spent in Brookline. These figures are based on average daily membership. To meet the diverse needs of white, black, Puerto Rican, and Oriental children, Boston should now have the resources to spend at least $1,500 per pupil to equalize educational opportunity. By the time Boston does spend that much, the higher income suburbs will be spending $1,800 or $2000 per pupil.

The state aid formula for education treats Boston like any other city in Massachusetts, although it assumes Boston has a higher property tax base than many other communities. The formula does not consider the extra money Boston must spend to provide police, fire, and sanitation services for the hundreds and thousands of suburban dwellers who work or shop in Boston each day. Economists call the extra burden and higher costs of city services "municipal overburden." The extra costs of educating the children of the poor, mainly in the inner-city section of Boston, is similarly a financial "educational overburden." The state aid formula should, therefore, add factors to recognize municipal overburden and funds to supplement federal aid for the disadvantaged.

In addition, since 1967, Boston has not received its fair share of federal funds through the state. State officials explain that Boston must submit proposals for each of the separate federal programs. Boston officials explain that these funds count against Boston schools in the 1963 aid formula which limits the school department's spending power. Both are correct.

Recommendations

- State officials should aggressively seek proposals (e.g., for occupational education) from the largest city in the state and should offer Boston technical and other services to help prepare proposals for all federal and state programs.
- Boston school officials should seek increased federal and state revenues for city programs.
- Either the statutory budget limit on Boston general school appropriations should be removed, or the formula factor which penalizes a school system for seeking federal revenues should be eliminated.

The city applied for and used most of the federal funds allocated for disadvantaged children. Nevertheless, despite almost 9 percent of the eligible children in the state, Boston received only 4 percent of the vocational education aid, 6 percent of the library aid, and 6 percent of the aid for science, math, guidance, and foreign language programs financed partly with federal funds.

The Advisory Commission on Intergovernmental Relations suggests that each state have a metropolitan educational equalization authority whose governing board would levy an area property tax and approve a distribution formula commensurate with each district's needs. Such a board in Greater Boston might serve an area roughly equivalent to the territory of the Metropolitan Area Planning Council. Not only Boston but Chelsea, Somerville, and other communities with limited tax bases would benefit from a formula based on property tax limitations which determines educational needs by family income levels, dropout rates, and achievement scores.

The state should also assume more responsibility for equitable property tax assessments and collections. The next master plan for Massachusetts taxation may include state supervision of assessment and state-wide property tax collection to guarantee equal treatment of property-owners as well as to retain a productive tax for other local services.

The state school aid formula for cities must be revised. The NESDEC (New England School Development Council) formula was developed early in the 1960s, before the war on poverty or the recognition of the effect of discrimination on blacks and Puerto Ricans. Dr. Charles S. Benson, principal consultant to NESDEC on the formula, later urged Rhode Island to adopt an aid formula based partly on property tax base factors and partly on the need to supplement Title I, ESEA funds based on family income. Massachusetts should adopt a formula which uses income level data to indicate ability to pay for education and need for education. The amount of education an individual has correlates well with average lifetime earnings. Income rises with education and individuals with low incomes often need more education to free them from poverty.

Recommendations

- Boston and state officials should plan for a minimum of 90 percent state financing of education by the middle or late seventies. Education will be financed by federal shared tax revenue and by a revised state income tax. The state should finance its share of the commissioner's EDUCARE proposal in the 1971 session. Federal officials should press for federal revenue sharing and for full financing of authorized urban programs.
- Massachusetts should revise the state aid formula to recognize municipal overburden and greater educational costs of central city school systems.
- The state should, even without aid formula revision, consider additional aid for disadvantaged children which has been based on family income. This should be the core of a system of "urban aid" grants to cities.

Many economists do not approve of certain categorical funds which are now available for transportation, lunches, construction of schools to reduce racial imbalance, vocational education, special education, and bilingual education. To an extent these distort decisions about allocation of funds. On the other hand, they represent genuine priorities which otherwise might be neglected in attempts to treat everyone equally. Equal opportunity requires more than merely spending the same amount of dollars for every student. It may require spending *extra* money on students who are handicapped—physically, emotionally or educationally—to raise them to the level of the rest of the population. The role of the state should be to pick up the excess costs but also to insist on effective use of state and local funds.

Additional state funds for education will simultaneously affect other decisions now made by the school committee:

- The state will eventually assume more responsibility for collective bargaining for public school employees. Employees and school officials will recognize the inefficiency and inequities of negotiating separate wage scales in each school system. They will continue to negotiate many working conditions locally.

- The state will insist on more adequate program evaluation. It is likely to insist on a program budgeting (PPBES) to review alternative proposals for additional funds.
- The state will undoubtedly modify state certification laws to provide a variety of instructional roles similar to the mixed staffing proposals in this report. The MACE study of certification directed by Lindley Stiles will provide the model.

Full, or nearly full, state financing of Boston schools eventually will render academic some of the immediate questions of the system's fiscal independence from the mayor. Given the current limitations of the mayor's role, he should have either much more power, or much less. With state financing, the mayor should no longer be blamed for school spending patterns or lack of funds. Boston should be treated as one of the 350 independent cities and towns whose school budgets cannot be cut but whose committee members can be removed if they waste taxpayer's money. The mayor should become less involved in school financial decision-making, as the Boston school system grows more dependent on the state.

The State Department of Education

Until the mid-1960s the State Department of Education concentrated its resources on rapidly growing districts and on smaller school districts which needed considerable state assistance. The larger cities and wealthy suburbs needed little state assistance; in fact, they paid their administrators and supervisors considerably more than the state specialists. Boston needed to confer with the state only on rare occasions, for example, about vocational education programs.

In 1970 more than half of Boston department directors ranked the state in the top three of the ten most important external relationships. Boston planners began to negotiate school construction proposals with buildings and racial imbalance specialists. Boston sought additional federal aid through state channels for library books, vocational education, program innovations, planning, and compensatory education.

As in most states, Massachusetts state officials—with few exceptions—represented rural or suburban backgrounds. Recent commissioners brought urban experience to the department, and visited Boston schools. The commissioner has encouraged his staff to work with Boston and has tried to recruit urban-experienced and urban-oriented staff members for service in the department. Staff members in 1970 were working with Boston on vocational education, special education, Model Cities programs and other projects.

The MACE Report on Pupil Services has called for a state bureau of pupil services, for state leadership of the pupil attendance function, and for transfer of pupil adjustment counselors from the Youth Services Board to education. The report calls for relaxation of the compulsory attendance law (ages 7-16) to allow work study and other out-of-school learning experiences. Furthermore, the state should provide models by which to evaluate pupil services policies, and it should provide consultants to improve pupil programs. The report recommends new ratios for pupil service staffing and urges using aides.

The MACE Report on Compensatory Education includes many recommendations for the state as well as training guidelines for colleges and universities. The report insists that the state play a stronger role in Title I proposal review, evaluation, and monitoring to insure that educators follow the intent of the statute. The state must add qualified program evaluators to its staff and insist on adequate short-term and long-term evaluation from school systems. At the same time, state officials must lobby nationally for more timely federal appropriations and for supplementary state and local funds for the economically disadvantaged children it does not now serve. Massachusetts was one of three states which enacted compensatory education before federal statutes appeared, but the state has subsequently accepted as sufficient the federal aid for this category.

The state has provided inadequate funding for other educational programs, including education of the academically talented, the arts, and humanities programs, and services for students with dyslexia, and other special needs. City children need this aid and city school systems require state incentives to finance these more expensive, but necessary programs. The state Board of Education must remind the governor and legislature of these commitments.

The state can play a central role in establishing school lunch programs for all city children by the mid-1970s. The state can provide technical assistance and help secure additional financial aid to make possible breakfast programs for many inner-city children whose diet does not meet minimum nutritional standards and whose ability to learn is therefore impaired. The same facilities may be shared by other agencies concerned with the elderly, some of whom would be able to work in the lunch program.

The state can provide leadership in the Boston metropolitan area which should benefit the city. The MACE report on the State Department of Education recommends a regional center for the Greater Boston area which should be in Boston or easily accessible.

The Boston area needs a media resources center for films, tapes, and specialized records and filmstrips. Boston students age 12 to 18 can help staff such a center not only as a prevocational opportunity but as an outlet for talent in film-making and electronics. Many metropolitan functions can be served effectively and economically even without a formal metropolitan school district. Four examples follow.

- The Boston School Committee has given enthusiastic support to EDCO, the Education Collaborative for Greater Boston, which is a prototype for regional state action involving the Boston, Brookline, Cambridge, Newton, suburban, diocesan, and independent schools. EDCO, with Boston and state support, has conducted workshops and intensive seminars for teachers on new media, human relations curriculum, China and world affairs, and elementary science. Some of the learning takes place through teacher exchange and school-to-school programs and a program of "small grants" to teachers who want to try out new courses and methods.

    EDCO, now a Title III project (ESEA), should continue in an expanded and more enduring form; its staff has proposed joint curriculum development for drug education, race relations, and the humanities. The EDCO Model deserves substantial state and federal financial support.

- The Metropolitan Council on Educational Opportunity, originally a Title III project and now largely supported by state funds, has extended to more than 1,000 black children in Boston the option of attending schools in suburban or other city districts. The state need not abolish suburban boundary lines or create a mammoth school district. It could offer additional incentives to Boston and to suburbs which build larger school plants to serve Boston children. Why not offer 85 percent construction aid rather than 65 percent for Boston *and* communities within a twenty-five mile radius willing to assist in reducing racial imbalance? Citizens must recognize that racial integration in the northeast is a suburban and metropolitan responsibility, not just an urban problem. State officials and citizens reviewing the Racial Imbalance Law should focus on the problems caused by planning few schools in minority group areas, especially in the South End and Roxbury. Perhaps partnership schools and variations of the magnet school (Trotter) could serve as alternative models. The effects of open enrollment and school staffing policies also must be reviewed periodically by the state.

- The state has an obligation to plan for the crisis in financing urban and metropolitan education. The commissioner has proposed an EDUCARE program which would provide one-third of the education funds from federal sources and one-third of the funds from the state. Boston needs EDUCARE revenue immediately. By 1976 the combined state and federal share should approach 90 percent of the total Boston budget, if only because many Boston residents are poor and not equipped to pay for their education. The state must raise substantially all of the funds necessary to equalize not only the tax base but the educational opportunities for city children. At the same time, the state should evaluate programs, personnel, and productivity as a return on the state investment.

    One side-effect, already predictable (although not yet at hand) is regional collective bargaining and perhaps eventual state-wide bargaining. Since 1965 many communities have had to negotiate harder each year just to keep their salary scale similar to nearby communities. The state might provide leadership to adjacent communities so that cities maintain a 10-15 percent edge on salaries, especially in high turnover schools, or secure additional experienced staff for such schools. Teacher unions and associations should join with the commissioner and his staff to plan equitable and economic ways to avoid excessive salary competitions and costly strikes and to plan positively for adequate incentives, compensation, training and staffing for all inner-city schools. A 1972 MACE study by Paul Cook recommended that the state set staffing ratios in order to equalize opportunity among school systems.

- The state must be the broker and disseminator of useful ideas and exemplary methods developed by experimental schools (with state support), especially Title III programs (many of which are suburban), the education component of Model Cities. The commissioner should convene a major conference on urban education to discuss model programs, analyze interagency collaboration required of health, education, housing, and other officials, review the needs of ethnic and minority groups, and continue discussion of recommendations in this report. This conference could have national visibility and could emphasize the need for concerted state executive and legislative action.

Linking Program Evaluation to the Budget

The components of an urban educational planning scheme, as discussed in Chapter 2,[a] constitute a program budgeting system which Boston should adopt. Program budgeting will encourage rational decision-making about resource allocation. And rational budget decision-making is both necessary and possible in the Boston Schools.

For most agencies a budget serves three functions: it presents a plan; lays out the program priorities; and makes possible a system of financial and administrative control. The present Boston school budget serves none of these functions. It is considered and revised months after the school year has begun, rewards employee-group activism, not educational priorities, and too frequently is ignored by committees which create new positions at will.

All levels of government currently are considering PPBES (Planning, Programming, Budgeting, Evaluation Systems) to examine program alternatives, make decisions, and manage systems properly. By 1975, federal, state, and even city aid to Boston schools may be tied to this type of budget format.

The implementation of modern planning in Boston depends on five factors:

1. The superintendent and the associate superintendent must support this approach and feel comfortable with its operation.
2. The superintendent must be willing to recruit specially trained personnel at all levels of the planning effort and to use outside consulting services.

---

[a]See "The Planning and Analysis of Educational Programs," Chapter 2.

3. Planning would proceed in a balanced fashion, stressing analysis, evaluation of effectiveness, performance monitoring, and genuine analysis of alternative proposals.
4. Organizational development and budgetary specialists would conduct a complete in-service training program for system personnel.
5. The superintendent and school committee must be willing to reorganize structurally important sections of the Boston School Department to facilitate collection of vital planning information and implementation of proposed programs.

By 1975, the school department should reorganize its staff, creating a Department of Planning, Management, and Evaluation (PME), and a Department of the Budget. These two departments would work closely together, but the central functions of analysis and evaluation would take place only in the Department of PME. The Department of the Budget would supply expert and up-to-date cost information, and it would assist in preparing the traditional budget, the program budget, the crosswalk between these two, required by the federal, state, and city governments, and the display of fiscal information. A separate analytic and review staff should *not* develop within the Department of the Budget..

Together, these departments would be the superintendent's management staff and would only be responsible to him. The deputy superintendent would carry out decisions that reflect recommendations from either department for changes in program and personnel. The two department heads and the deputy super-intendent would be the superintendent's inner-staff advisory council. The other members of what is now the board of superintendents, with this inner council, would be a central advisory board. The head of PME would have primary responsibility for presenting program changes, and the head of the budget would support his recommendations. One of the major tasks of the budget adminis-trator would be to insure financial adherence to program decisions. Two chief assistants—one for program accounting and documentation, another for budget control—would help him complete these tasks.

The Department of PME would comprise personnel involved in planning, management, and evaluation at the central and district levels. Functionally, it would be divided into five areas: analysis, control, evaluation, data processing, and organizational development. This department should include twenty-five planners at the central level. In addition, it should supply twelve planners on a rotating basis to districts and, on demand, to individual schools to develop proposals for review by the central analysis group. The personnel of this department will total thirty-seven, excluding the staff of the data-processing center.

After consulting with the Department of the Budget and with associate superintendents, the Department of PME at the central office level would make recommendations including: the size of the city's school budget; the number, size, and composition of school system districts; allocation of funds among school districts; provision and availability of special services; integration plans; school construction plans; job specifications for negotiating with unions; performance standards for which districts are accountable; program evaluation; reporting and control; and system-wide data processing requirements.

At the area level, the Department of PME would help teachers, principals, councils, and superintendents develop proposals for: allocations among buildings; allocations among programs and grade levels; assessing the special needs of student populations by attendance area, building, etc.; using state and federal funds; community involvement in the schools; integrating high school and elementary curricula; negotiating with unions on items peculiar to the district; a district program and financial plan; program evaluation, and many other areas.

Districts would have some authority to allocate funds within the district. These allocations must conform with central office guidelines and districts must submit to review of their decisions.

The Department of PME would include an associate superintendent for planning, management, and evaluation who has five to ten years experience in planning and management. He should have a doctorate, and should be familiar with the methodologies of evaluation, cost-effectiveness, and management information and reporting systems. He might have worked in an educational corporation like Xerox or General Learning, in government, or even in an action-oriented community development enterprise at the national level.

There would also be directors with research and management experience relevant to their particular units. They might have been planners in Boston, in other school systems, or in industry. A master's degree would be the minimum required, although a doctorate would be preferable.

Finally, there would be departmental planners skilled in subject-matter disciplines and in management. They should have at least three, preferably five, years of experience in their particular field.

Creating a Department of Planning, Management, and Evaluation would require substantial strengthening of the educational data-processing department. The programming staff would be increased from four to ten or fifteen. Over five years, the staff would expand from six to twenty. Average salary for programmers (currently $10,000) would increase to $16,000-18,000 during three years.

The Data Processing Center would expand its focus from pupil accounting and budgetary services to meet the data requirements of the analysis and evaluation units of the Department of PME.

The Educational Planning Center would be absorbed by the new department. Because the Educational Planning Center is too understaffed to cope with the projected work load of the Department of PME and because it lacks many capabilities necessary to complete PME tasks, it would be redesigned to conform with new departmental specifications. It would also include outside personnel from industry and government.

The Planning and Analysis of Educational Programs

Traditionally, school system planning is designed to meet present needs and to deal with perceived needs of the immediate future. But it seldom meets these needs. It tends to be episodic and short-sighted about the long-range effects of plans and about their impact on other school system components. Moreover, this sort of planning is based on input. It usually focuses on creating new resources or in increasing the level of resources currently used in executing existing programs. Modern planning techniques are different in three ways.

First, modern planning involves a consideration of alternative schemes. Modern planning technique alone does not see a plan as sufficient response to system needs. Instead, it urges developing many different plans to achieve the desired end and using systems analysis to evaluate their relative utilities. A particular plan's usefulness often emerges as one examines the resources necessary for the plan against the plan's projected effectiveness.

Second, modern planning has both an input and an output dimension. Modern planning concentrates not only on inputs or resources but also on the outputs or results of plans that have been implemented. This broader concept of planning is sometimes called output planning, or planning for accountability.

Third, modern planning considers plans and their effects throughout the system and over time. Planning in the past was simply a response to system needs. Therefore the resulting plan focused only on the problem that had initially generated attention. The modern planner, however, wants to know not only what accepting and implementing a plan will mean in other parts of the existing system, but also what using a plan will mean fiscally and otherwise over a ten-year period.

Modern planning, then, is based on cost-effectiveness analysis of several plans designed to achieve a rationally defined objective; the plans' anticipated and actual performances; and the calculated long-range effects each plan will have on the entire system. This approach is Planning-Programming-Budgeting.

A planning facility for the Boston school system should have seven basic parts.

1. Structural analysts would define problems and outline objectives for the decision-makers.
2. Analysts would consider primarily the more analytic portion of modern planning.
3. Administrators would monitor and observe the implementation of approved plans.
4. Evaluative analysts would assess and report the final performance of programs semiannually.
5. Data-processing personnel would provide information for those involved in management reporting and program analysis.

6. Organizational development personnel would train people and try to insure that system personnel understand, accept, and cooperate with the planning effort.
7. Budgetary analysts would coordinate the mechanics and processes of the traditional budget with innovative program account approaches.

The first concern of these people would be to build a program structure to categorize the ongoing activities of the entire school system on at least five levels, beginning with the school system and continuing through the major program divisions of the system—instructional programs, general support programs. The organizational pattern of the system would determine the following levels of the program structure. (One level might include activities for each of the districts within the system and other levels might provide information on individual schools and specific activities.) The structural analysts would examine various program structures to identify those that would facilitate analysis. They would assist the budgetary analysts to cost out by program structure level the resources expended in various activities. Finally, the structural analysts would define broad goals and specific objectives and coordinate them with program activities.

The more analytic planners would examine alternative processes or programs designed to carry out the objectives the structural analysts have set; but their particular responsibility would be to explore alternative designs for new programs. In this context, the analytic planner would work closely with the budgetary analyst to cost out program changes and new programs, rank alternatives based on cost-effectiveness analyses, and prepare recommendations for the head of school system planning.

The planning administrators would prepare reports for the head of planning and advise the analytic staff about planning progress.

The evaluative analysts would conduct studies and collect data on the final program results.

The data-processing components should service all three tiers of an urban school system—the central, district, and individual school levels—but its main responsibility to the planning group would be developing computer programs to provide data directly relevant to planning needs.

Organizational development personnel would implement plans and reduce resistance of personnel by involving them in the planning process. This group would also help the structural analysts set accurate objectives at the central, district, and school levels and accompany administrators who observe programs in the schools to insure reliable interim evaluation. OD personnel would evaluate how the school system functions in relation to its goals.

The main function of the budgetary analysts would be to account for programs at all levels and to advise analytic planners about the fiscal feasibility of the alternatives considered.

None of these components—and no part of the planning cycle—could operate in isolation; each makes material contributions and becomes indispensable to the others. As implementation proceeded, different components would take the main roles—structural analysts during the developmental stage, analytic planners when the system was fully operative, and budgetary analysts during the preparation of the program budget. Communication would have to be well-developed among the different components at all times.[3]

Ideas on the implementation of program planning, evaluation, and budgeting will appear later in the report.

Costs

Once it is fully operative, the Department of Planning, Management, and Evaluation could cost approximately $1,000,000 annually. This figure absorbs the costs of several current departments. The research and evaluation unit of the Department of Title I Programs currently spends about $75,000 annually. The Departments of Educational Investigation and Measurement, of Statistics, and of Data Processing spend $285,000, $35,000, and $278,000, respectively. The new department may effect economies by using personnel more efficiently and by eliminating activities that do not contribute directly to system and district planning or to school services. Yet the Department of PME would require relatively expensive planning personnel brought in from industry and government, especially at the higher administrative levels. But given Boston's current $80,000,000 school budget and the anticipated increase in that figure, $1,000,000 (1.25 percent of the current budget) is not too much to spend for the activities of the existing departments as well as the comprehensive services of the new department.

The additional cost of the Department of PME's first year of operation is uncertain. It would fall, however, between $100,000 and $200,000, depending on the difficulties of organizing the new department, implementing the planning system, and recruiting qualified personnel from outside the school system.

Implementation

The first major task for the Department of PME would be to design a plan for program budgeting for the Boston Public Schools. The first two years would require training personnel at all levels, and the organizational development unit of PME would be responsible both for this effort and for setting objectives. No one can install PPBES suddenly and uniformly in a large urban school system. It must be implemented slowly by the Department of PME.

Consultants and Outside Help

The early stages of reorganizing the school system's planning capability and of implementing formal PPBES require consultants who would continue to be useful throughout the planning process. Eventually, their roles would become advisory for the school system cannot substitute consulting services for the development of in-house capabilities.

Still, consultants would be necessary, and the system might want to let contracts for planning functions beyond the current abilities of system personnel. Boston should select consultants carefully; both the superintendent's administrative staff and the Department of PME should oversee their selection. The school department should award consultants' contracts on a continuing basis rather than an annual one.

This report recommends first, a reorganization of the school system's planning capability that involves an expanded interpretation of planning and second, an approach for implementing a program budgeting system in Boston. These efforts will require energy and funds. But their completion should produce better decisions about resource allocation in the Boston system.

Notes

1. SCHOOL MANAGEMENT, January 1968, p. 122.

2. STATE AID TO LOCAL GOVERNMENT, Report A-34, April 1969, The Advisory Commission on Intergovernmental Relations (an official board of state, county, local, and federal officials).

3. See S.A. Haggert, "Considerations in Developing a Program Budgeting System," PROGRAM BUDGETING FOR SCHOOL DISTRICT PLANNING, CONCEPTS AND APPLICATIONS (RAND Corporation, Santa Monica, California; November 1969; Memorandum #RM-6116-RC), pp. 185-94.

 **The Alternatives to
School System Change**

If Boston schools, or schools in other cities, do not respond to demands for change, local school officials should expect that the state and federal governments will finance alternative efforts to make education more productive:

- The state could finance a network of experimental schools which are more willing to provide new curricula, minority staff leadership and considerable citizen involvement. The new CCED (Community Council for Educational Development) school is one of three already authorized by the legislature and State Board of Education.
- The federal government might expand a pilot effort to test a voucher plan whereby parents can select a public or independent school of their choice as long as it meets state standards and admits all races. The state will reimburse each school, according to how many vouchers the school collects. In the 1970s, the Office of Economic Opportunity will sponsor this experiment in various communities in the nation.
- State and federal governments will contract out educational programs to business firms, community development corporations, hospitals, museums, and other agencies. The grants will provide for manpower training, teacher training, curriculum development, and other educational efforts—including the development of new kinds of schools. Federal and state officials have already made grants like these, in some cases so that a city would not lose needed funds because a school system had not submitted a proposal.

At this time, Boston already has alternate or separate educational programs. Agencies need one another. Hospitals and schools must pool facilities, staff, and expertise to develop student interest and skills. Several agencies and centers other than school systems can develop the kinds of curriculum materials teachers want and need. School systems may aspire to be fiscally and educationally independent, but the social system is too complex and education too expensive to tolerate duplication of effort on many fronts.

On the other hand, competition and even conflict over funding, priorities, and success are American customs. Systems without competition and controversy grow complacent and unresponsive. Schools should compete vigorously for resources. Leaders cannot waste time and energy defending programs which are not sufficiently useful, challenging, and responsive to the needs of the future. Television educates, churches educate, museums educate, and community groups educate. This pluralism is healthy, a source of strength for *all* education.

Boston school officials have recognized the educative value in museums, symphonies, newspapers, distributive education, and many other programs. These and other alliances suggested in this report must be strengthened as the needs of children and of the country grow more complex in the decades ahead. Boston school officials must visit and observe closely the new community schools and CCED schools, the New England Hospital and Urban League programs, the Parkway Program of Philadelphia, and other efforts that reach out for the rich resources of great cities.

Urban School Improvement—Whose Responsibility?

Every state and national legislator, and every individual—the governor or a private citizen—is responsible for improving public education in Boston.

In the past, federal and state policies encouraged more and better housing in suburbia than in the cities, financed fast highways on which to flee the city, and provided tax exemptions for institutions that require a major urban setting. Now the tide must turn. Urban school systems must have substantial additional revenues to help the diverse populations living in the city. Increased state and federal aid is needed to pay for expensive urban services.

As education improves, so must urban health and housing programs. The recommendations in this report depend on a network of neighborhood or community health services and on substantially greater public investment in mental health services.

At the same time, it is poor public policy to build huge housing projects which concentrates low income students in one school. Mixing the types of housing might provide greater diversity and possibly higher student achievement in the classroom.

The greatest aid for education would be the elimination of poverty, an objective within the reach of national policy-makers if they consider an adequate income maintenance or family allowance program. It is extraordinarily difficult to teach children who are undernourished, whose families lack adequate clothing and shelter, and whose interest in education is eclipsed by more immediate problems of survival. One can correlate a minimum family income with the likelihood of success in bringing poor children into the society through education.

The survey of Boston revealed that administrators recognize the important role of the state. Since 1965, state influence on the city has increased substantially because of the Racial Imbalance Law, Public Employee Negotiations and other legislation on bilingual and special education. Despite the surge of interest in home rule and restructuring urban government by local commissions, education traditionally has been a state function. If cities will not or cannot respond to challenges—educationally, organizationally, financially—then the state constitution formally charges the Commonwealth of Massachusetts with the responsibility. Citizens will continue to look to the state for relief and for the redress of grievances that are not resolved at the local level.

And if our cities are to remain exciting and adaptable, the state must respond. Yet in too many capitol cities, the local schools enjoy less than outstanding reputations because too few people care, speak up, and organize to present their concerns.

Writing a report doesn't always lead to action. Reports serve as blueprints and guidelines for the makers of public policy. Others must act:

- The School Committee can approve most of the recommendations concerning school policies and departments and can strengthen the roles of principals and area superintendents.
- The Mayor and Council must consider ideas to make the school committee more representative of the city, and must act on many of the recommendations concerning health facilities, parks, and related services.
- The Superintendent and his staff must administer the reorganization and work to see that procedures change, that new responsibilities are assumed, and that new talent is recruited for the difficult work of planning, evaluation, and accounting for progress.
- The Governor, State Board and Commissioner, and the General Court must redouble their efforts to assist the largest cities—indeed all the cities of the Commonwealth—in organizing effectively to meet the general needs of all children and the special needs of minorities. This means channeling much more money to the cities than to the suburbs—a reversal of what seemed necessary in the 1940s and 1950s.

Local citizens, individually or in groups, must insist on frequent progress reports from officials about action on the recommendations of this report and on urban education generally. If neighborhood groups, teacher groups, or local school faculties remain silent, one assumes that they are satisfied with the current status of the schools. If fewer than half the citizens vote in local elections, this suggests either ignorance or arrogance about matters that affect Massachusetts and the quality of life in this region. Every voter must exercise his right to select those who organize and maintain an urban school system to meet the diverse needs of Boston citizens.

Index

Milieu therapy, 122
Mixed staffing, 48-49, 50
Model Cities Administration, 45
Model Cities program, 47, 51, 156-159
Model Neighborhood Boards, 45
Model schools, 35, 36
Museum of Fine Arts, 138, 139, 140, 141

National Defense Education Act, 19
National Teachers Examination, 61, 69, 77
Negotiation, 73, 182
Neighborhood Health Clinics, 113-114, 115
New England Association of Colleges and Secondary Schools, 16
New England Hospital (Roxbury), 109
New England Merchant's Bank, 144
New England Mutual Life Insurance Company, 144
New England Telephone Company, 101, 144
New schools, planning, 157-158
Nonpublic schools, 91
Nurses, school, 118, 121

Occupational education, 105-110
Occupational Resource Center, 108, 152
Occupations, trends in, 105
Office of Staff and Organizational Development, 69
Ombudsman, 59, 175
Open enrollment, 57
Operation Counterpoise, 22, 101, 125
Operation Second Chance, 125
Organization Development Workshop, 80
Organizational development, personnel for, 189
Organizations, parents', 43-45, 50-51

Paperwork, problem of, 29, 32
Paraprofessionals, 122, 141
Parents, 1-12, 46-53
  concerns and opinions of, 1-12
  influence of, 43-46, 77
  involvement of, 21, 46-53, 155, 156
  organizations of, 43-45, 50-51
  Park and Recreation Department, 153-154
Parkway Program, 89

Parochial schools, closing of, 90-92
Participation:
  parent, 21
  in planning, 88-89
  student, 54-56
Partnership schools, 47, 57, 158
Pay-period, 34
Personnel:
  administrative, 34
  Boards, 65
  department of, 84
  function, 76-77
  hiring freeze, 171
  problems, 169-170
  −student ratio, 120
Physical examinations, 112-113
Planning, 40-, 78-79, 126-127, 129, 188
  advocate, 89
  facility for, 188-190
  implementation of, 185-186, 190-191
  lack of, 13
  new schools, 150-152, 157-158
  problems of, 88-96
  responsibility for, 75, 78-79, 83-84
Planning, Programming, Budgeting, Evaluation System (PPBES), 129, 175, 182, 185, 190-191
Planners, 187, 189
Polaroid Corporation, 144
Policy handbook, 23
Principals, 27, 29, 34, 58
  responsibilities of, 14, 19, 27, 31-35, 62, 157
  selection of, 36, 65, 155
Priorities, 9, 176
Problem areas, xvii-xviii
Problems, 14, 88-96, 114, 117-119, 122, 128, 169-170
Program for Children with Learning Problems, 159
Programmers, 187
Programs, 13-15
  collaborative, 138-147
Psychiatrists, 122, 123
Psychologists, 120, 122
Public Facilities Department (PFD), 151, 152
Public relations, 132
Pupil adjustment counselor, 96, 118, 119, 122
Pupil services, 85

About the Authors

Joseph M. Cronin is Secretary of Educational Affairs for the Commonwealth of Massachusetts. He has taught school, been a principal, and was at the Harvard Graduate School of Education a lecturer, professor and Associate Dean. Between 1964 and 1970 he participated in or directed studies of the Boston schools for the U.S. Office of Education, City of Boston, State of Massachusetts, Carnegie and Danforth Foundations. He has written THE CONTROL OF URBAN SCHOOLS and other books and reports on city schools.

Richard M. Hailer is Assistant Secretary of Educational Affairs in Massachusetts. A former science teacher, he served as a Peace Corps volunteer and administrator on three continents. He worked for the Behavioral Science Center (later McBer Co.) as a consultant and study administrator. His special interests include program development, bilingual education, personnel management, organizational development and renewal. He has consulted with many states, countries, and community action agencies. In 1970 he was Associate Director of the Boston School Study.